HISTORY OF MICHIGAN,

FROM ITS EARLIEST COLONIZATION TO THE PRESENT TIME.

BY JAMES H. LANMAN

NEW YORK:
HARPER & BROTHERS, PUBLISHERS,
329 & 331 PEARL STREET,
FRANKLIN SQUARE.
1852.

PREFACE.

The design of this volume is to present to the reader, in a brief and popular form, a view of the principal events connected with the history, progress, and present condition of Michigan, condensed from the larger work prepared by the author under the sanction of a law of that State. Such a work, embracing a great variety of particulars relating to the early settlement and subsequent growth of the West, would, it was thought, be both useful and interesting. The rapid advance of the vast territory bordering on the lakes in population and wealth, is the best commentary on the nature and effects of our free institutions, and offers a political phenomenon well worthy of being studied.

For my facts I have relied principally upon Father Marquette, Hennepin, Joutel, La Hontan, Charlevoix, Rogers, Henry, Carver, M'Kenzie, Bouchette, and M'Gregor, and have consulted with particular care Mr. Bancroft's great work, the "History of the Colonization of the United States." The discourses, also, which have from time to time been delivered before the Michigan Historical Society, by Cass, Schoolcraft, Whiting, and Biddle, I found full of valuable information. Nor must I omit to acknowledge the great obligations I am under to my friend Mr. Schoolcraft, for his kindness in permitting me to consult his library, which is especially rich in everything relating to the West, as freely as if it had been my own. Besides these means of information, a residence in the interior of the state for a considerable period has afforded me a knowledge of its actual condition, which could not, perhaps, have been obtained in any other way.

If in this work, prepared during the intervals of professional labour, I shall have succeeded in presenting an impartial history of this interesting State, and in a manner to entertain and instruct the intelligent reader, my object will have been fully accomplished.

J. H. L.

New-York, August 18th, 1841.

CONTENTS.

CHAPTER I.

General Description of the State.—Soil.—Minerals.—Streams—Interior Lakes.—The Great Lakes.—Origin of their Names.—Wild Animals.—Birds.—Fish.—Counties . . Page 15

CHAPTER II.

First Advance of the Missionaries to the Lakes.—Brebœuf—Daniel—Pijart—Charles Raymbault.—First bark Canoe of white Men reaches St. Mary.—Father Jaques—Bressani—Chaumonotot—Claude Dablon—Mesnard—Lallemand—Gabrieile Dreuillette, and Leonard Gareau.—Réné Mesnard advances to Che-goi-me-gon.—Father Claude Allouez.—Father James Marquette.—Indian Council held at the Falls of St. Mary.—Marquette's Explorations.—His Death.—Robert de la Salle—His Explorations.—Michilimackinac founded.—Death of La Salle.—Sault de Ste. Marie.—Fort St. Joseph.—Detroit founded.—Its early Condition.—Attacked by the Ottawas.—By the Foxes.—Early French Travellers through the Lakes 32

CHAPTER III.

Colonial Emigrants.—Merchants.—Coureurs des Bois.—The Peasantry.—French Soldiers.—Legal Administration.—Policy of the French Government.—Indian Mythology of the Lakes.—Mode of Land Distribution.—Increase of Colonization.—The Fur-trade of the Lakes.—Canadian Boat-songs.—La Hontan's Account of the Fur-trade . . . 78

CHAPTER IV.

Struggle between France and England for the Possession of the Country.—The Iroquois and Algonquins.—British Troops advance into Canada.—Battle of Quebec.—Death of Wolfe and Montcalm.—British Detachment under Rogers takes Possession of Michigan.—Rogers traverses Lake Erie.—Pontiac makes his first Appearance.—Bellestre.—Surrender of Detroit . . . . Page 96

CHAPTER V.

Condition of the Territory under the English—Pontiac forms a Confederacy to attack the English Posts.—War breaks out. —Siege of Detroit.—Battle of Bloody Bridge.—Indians assemble around Michilimackinac.— Minavavana — Alexander Henry —Wawatam.—Michilimackinac destroyed. — General Bradstreet arrives.—Peace concluded.—Death of Pontiac 118

CHAPTER VI.

Condition of the Fur-trade under the English.—Hudson's Bay Company.—English Administration of the Law.—Criminal Trial.—Quebec Act.—Mineral Rock on Lake Superior.—Northwest Company.—American Revolution.—Expeditions from Detroit.—Indian Council held at Detroit.—American Independence established 145

CHAPTER VII.

Northwestern Territory organized.—Arthur St. Clair appointed Governor.—English refuse to surrender the Posts.—Indian Disaffection.—Indian Council at Detroit.—Message from the Spanish Settlements on the Banks of the Mississippi.—Campaign of General Harmar.—Campaign of General St. Clair.—Campaign of General Wayne.—Extension of French Settlements.—Michigan surrendered to the United States.—Condition of the Territory in connexion with the Fur-trade.—Currency employed in the Fur-trade . . 163

CHAPTER VIII.

Condition of Michigan after the Surrender of the Posts.—Its Erection into a Territory.—General Hull appointed Governor. —Detroit destroyed by Fire.—Administration of the Law.—Third Indian Confederacy under Tecumseh and the Prophet. —Le Marquoit.—Land-office established.—Walk-in-the-Water.—Population in 1811.—Memorial from Michigan praying Aid from the General Government.—Savage Outbreak.—Operations on the Wabash.—American Fur Company Page 181

CHAPTER IX.

War declared between Great Britain and the United States.—Representations of Governor Hull.—Appointed to Command the Western Army.—Crosses to Sandwich and Addresses the Canadians.—Policy of Prevost.—Surrender of Detroit.—Tecumseh.—Conduct of Hull.—Expedition to the River Raisin.—Capture of Chicago.—Battle of the River Raisin.—General Harrison's Campaign.—Commodore Perry.—His Victory on Lake Erie.—General Harrison arrives at Malden. —Marches to Detroit.—Battle of the Thames.—Death of Tecumseh.—His Character.—Attack on Mackinaw.—Peace Concluded 197

CHAPTER X.

Lewis Cass appointed Governor of the Territory.—Its Condition at that Time.—Public Lands brought into Market.—First Steamboat on the Lakes.—University Founded.—Expedition to Explore the Lakes.—The Clinton Canal.—Mr. Porter appointed Governor.—Mode of making Surveys.—Controversy with Ohio.—Mr. Mason elected Governor.—State Organized. —Internal Improvements.—Education.—Conclusion . 228

APPENDIX.

First Colonization of Canada . . . . . . Page 249
Massacre of the Jesuits 252
Early Grant at Detroit 253
Early Land Trespass 257
Treaty of Greenville 258
General Hull's Proclamation 267

HISTORY OF MICHIGAN.

CHAPTER I.

General Description of the State.—Soil.—Minerals.—Streams.—Interior Lakes.—The Great Lakes.—Origin of their Names.—Wild Animals.—Birds.—Fish.—Counties.

THE State of Michigan derives its name, it is said, from the Indian words *Mitchi-sawgyegan*, which mean, in English, a great lake, a term which has been given to the territory from the position it occupies. It is bounded on the north by Lake Superior, on the south by Ohio and Indiana, on the east by Lake Erie, Lake St. Clair, and Lake Huron, and on the west by Lake Michigan, all of which lakes pour their accumulated waters down the Falls of Niagara. The extent of its domain is believed to be about sixty-five thousand square miles.

Along the shores of Lake Erie there stretches a belt of level and heavily-timbered land, bearing a growth of large and noble forest-trees upon a low and level soil. The land gradually rises towards the centre of the state, presenting a variegated scenery composed of tracts of dense wilderness, alternated with prairies, natural parks, or oak openings, copses of burr-oak, marshes, barrens, and pine groves, each watered by small streams, lakes, or springs. That part of the state which borders Lake Superior is more bold and primitive, and is broken by mountains and plains, hills and valleys. The Porcupine Mountains, which are the dividing ridge, and separate the waters of Lake Superior and Lake Michigan, are estimated at their most elevated point to be nearly two thousand feet high. Many parts exhibit a bold, rocky, and steril prospect, which caused one of the early French travellers, La Hontan, to call this region "the fag-end of the world." It abounds with forests of white and yellow pine, and will probably never be favourable for agricultural production, although it is a rich mineral region. The northwestern portion of the state is impressed with still more sublime features of natural scenery, comprising masses of stupendous rocks and rugged mountain chains; the northern part of the lower peninsula is flat, containing many swamps; the central portion is gently rolling, covered with groves of oak, alternated with tracts of heavily-timbered land, is peculiarly favourable for the production of wheat, which is its staple product, and presents the most picturesque points of scenery, and resources for the most dense population.

The soil of Michigan is various in its character. It is in general much more level than that of New-York and New-England, being of alluvial formation, and comparatively free from rocks. The different species of soil consist of heavily-timbered land, oak openings, burr-oak plains, prairies, and pine groves, each of which will be considered.

The heavily-timbered land consists of tracts which are densely wooded with a variety of large forest-trees, the principal of which are the black and white walnut, oaks of different species, maple, ash, elm, linden, sycamore, hackberry, cottonwood, aspen, locust, butternut, box or dogwood, poplar, whitewood, beech, cherry, sassafras, white, yellow, and Norway pine, hemlock, spruce, tamerack, cedar, cypress, chestnut, and pawpaw; as well as the smaller trees and shrubs, such as willow, alder, sumach, and honeysuckle, together with the different kinds of undergrowth which are found in the Middle and Southern States. This timbered land is often found upon the borders of the streams, upon what are called *bottoms*, and also upon the ridges which border them. It is discovered along the shores of the lakes from Monroe to Detroit, and thence to Lake Michigan, in a belt varying from five to fifteen miles in breadth. But a small proportion of the peninsular part of the state is, however, densely wooded.

There are various other species of soil which constitute a beautiful variety, and which will be described in their proper order. The soil which is heavily timbered is generally composed of a deep vegetable mould, sometimes mingled with clay, and produces a dense and luxuriant vegetation. Compared with the other sections of the state, it is gloomy, being generally more low and level, and it is more difficult to clear from the thick and tangled mass of trees which covers it; but these disadvantages are made up by its fertility, and it yields in great abundance the grasses, oats, buckwheat, potatoes, rye, and large crops of corn. Perhaps it is not so favourable to wheat, being damp, from the fact that it is shut out from the sun, and also cold in its nature.

In advancing into the interior of the state, across the narrow belt before described, we arrive upon a more dry and undulating soil — a species of land which swells into little hills like artificial mounds, and is called oak openings. This land is composed of a sandy loam, mingled sometimes with limestone pebbles, and appears light upon the surface, but, when laid open by the plough, turns black from the intermixture of lime in its composition. The trees, consisting chiefly of white-oak, scattered over the ground generally from ten to sixty feet apart, and extending for miles like cultivated parks, now sweeping down to a clear stream, a fertile prairie, or the brow of a transparent lake, impress one with the idea that he is travelling through an old, rather than a newly-settled country. These openings constitute a feature which distinguishes this from most of the adjoining states. The land, although not as productive as some other kinds of soil, yields heavy crops of oats and abundant harvests of wheat, besides the ordinary products of the Middle States. Although containing apparently but a thin covering of decomposed vegetable matter, the absence of that material is made up by the admixture of lime in its composition, which is favourable to vegetation ; and in summer the surface is almost entirely covered with red, yellow, white, and purple flowers, which, in their richness and beauty, are not known in the older-settled portions of the country, spreading a gorgeous carpet through the forest as far as the eye can reach. The surface of the oak openings also presents a turf of matted grass, which requires three or four yoke of oxen to break it up ; and, as you can ride for miles in a carriage under the trees that are thus widely separated, it does not need so great an amount of labour in clearing it as the timbered land. The trees, however, are usually girdled in order to effect their decay. These oak openings extend throughout the greater part of the lower peninsula.

Another species of soil of very great value is found in the state, commencing at the county of Jackson and studding the timbered land and oak openings from the head of the Kalamazoo River to the shores of Lake Michigan. It is called *burr-oak plains* or openings; a soil which consists of tracts spread over with groves of trees of a small size, called the burr-oak, with a rough bark and deep green foliage. They closely resemble cultivated orchards of pear-trees, springing from a soil which is composed of a brown loam mingled with clay; yet they are highly productive, and are deemed by the settlers of the greatest value, yielding in abundance the crops of the Middle States, corn, oats, potatoes, buckwheat, rye, and all the products of the other kinds of soil. As the trees, like those of the white-oak openings, are widely separated, this land requires but little clearing; but four or five yoke of oxen are generally used to break it up for seeding. Corn to the amount of forty, and sometimes eighty bushels to the acre, is produced from these openings, and from forty to fifty bushels of oats. Thirty bushels of wheat to the acre are also frequently obtained from this land; but the average amount may be placed at about twenty-five bushels.

Scattered through the south and southwestern part, particularly upon the borders of the Kalamazoo, the Grand, and St. Joseph Rivers, are what are called prairies. These consist of a soil destitute of trees, and covered with a deep surface of black sand and vegetable mould. It is more productive than any other species, yielding very large crops of corn and potatoes, as well as wheat, which is, however, apt not to be as clean as that on the openings. All other crops that are produced in this climate it yields in great profusion. These prairies throughout the state are comparatively small, but in Illinois they stretch out beyond the horizon like a sea. Being comparatively easy to cultivate, and producing so abundantly, they are always selected by the farmers before any other kind of soil. The dry prairies on the banks of the Kalamazoo and St. Joseph Rivers furnish a soil equal to any other in the West, and frequently from thirty to fifty bushels of corn have been raised upon them the first season, without being ploughed or hoed; and when the mould has been once subdued, from thirty to eighty bushels of corn, or forty of wheat, have been obtained to the acre; they are also very favourable for grass.

Another species of soil found in the state is called *wet prairies* or *marshes*, tracts which are generally in part or in whole covered with water;

and they produce a long and coarse grass that is very favourable for winter stock, and make a fine ranging ground for horses and cattle in the spring. When drained, these wet prairies may be converted into valuable meadow land.

Another species of soil that we meet with in the interior is termed *barrens*. They consist of tracts which are sparsely scattered over with stunted oaks or bushes, that would seem to indicate that the land is not favourable to vegetation. It is found, however, that by cultivation it produces well.

The kind of soil which is called *swamp* or *marsh land* is found in considerable tracts in the greater part of the state. It is in winter covered with water, and has a deep mire, which is dangerous to the traveller, and is sprinkled here and there with a few scattering trees or groves of tamerack, which resemble pine. In many cases these marshes are caused by beaver-dams.

The mineral productions of the state are various, and some of considerable value. Although the soil of the lower peninsula is, as has been before remarked, of alluvial formation, yet there are occasionally seen ledges of sandstone, which abounds in parts of the counties of Hillsdale, Jackson, Calhoun, Kalamazoo, Livingston, Ingham, Eaton, Barry, Shiawassee, Clinton, and other portions of the state. Gray limestone is also found; and on the immediate shore of Lake Huron a greenish-coloured clay slate has been discovered. Indications of coal are apparent in the counties of Eaton, Ingham, and Shiawassee. On the banks of the Grand River, near the Grand Rapids, beds of gypsum or plaster occur, which will be of considerable importance. Salt-springs, which can be used for the manufacture of salt, are scattered throughout a considerable portion of the interior ; and clay, sand, marl, bog iron ore, with other kinds, and springs tinctured with mineral qualities, especially sulphur, have been discovered in the eastern part of the peninsula, that may be of advantage for medicinal purposes.

Along the shores of Lake Superior, which are rich in mineral wealth, there are evidences of pure copper, and a large mass of that metal, near the mouth of the Ontonagon River, of many thousand pounds' weight, has excited the interest of travellers from the earliest period. Among the rocks on this part of the coast are also scattered prase, jaspar, carnelian, agate, sardonyx, and other rare stones of some value.

The greater part of the state is also well watered by numerous rivers and small streams, which variegate the landscape, and flow into the surrounding lakes. The principal of these are the Raisin, Grand River, the Kalamazoo, the St. Joseph, the Huron, the Clinton, the Saginaw, and the Ontonagon. The Detroit, the St. Clair, and the St. Mary's cannot be properly called rivers, as they are only straits which connect the lakes in the eastern and more level portions. Upon the eastern border of the state the rivers are sluggish, but, as you advance into the interior, they become more clear and rapid. The St. Joseph is a transparent and beautiful, though shallow stream, which meanders through the western part of the state over a bed of limestone rock and pebbles, and, watering counties of great fertility, consisting of oak lands and prairies, flows into Lake Michigan. The Kalamazoo is also a clear but narrow river, that runs over a surface of sand, limestone rock, or pebbles, and, watering extensive and productive tracts of the state, empties into the same lake. The Grand River is the largest stream in the interior, and, after furnishing a convenient channel for navigation and large manufacturing advantages, empties into Lake Michigan at Grand Haven. There are various other streams of less importance, which furnish sites for manufacturing establishments, and eligible points for settlement on their banks.

Another peculiar point in the scenery is the little lakes which are scattered over the soil. These are clear, and abound with fish; and in summer, when the vegetation upon their banks is in full bloom, appear like mirrors, where Nature, dressed in green and flowery robes, may admire her own beauty amid the solitude.

But the most prominent feature of the state is the great lakes which wash its shores. These constitute much the largest body of fresh water on the face of the globe. To the eye they appear like oceans, and water the borders of the forest for thousands of miles, from the state of New-York to the regions of Canada lying along the shores of Lake Superior, which are now ranged only by tribes of Indians and fur traders. Their surges roll like those of the sea, and the mariner obliged to navigate them often encounters as dangerous storms as upon the ocean. Their waters, however, are not, like those of the open sea, of a blue colour, but have a tinge of green, from the fact that they are fresh. They were formerly explored only by the bark canoes of the Indians, and were the theatre of the fur trade, which will be described hereafter; but, with the exception of Lake Superior, they are now crossed by steamboats of large tonnage, as well as vessels and ships of all sizes.

The origin of the names of the great lakes is not wanting in interest. Lake Ontario was formerly called Lake Frontenac, while that of Erie is derived from a nation of Erries, who roamed along the northern borders of Ohio, and were destroyed by the Iroquois. Lake Huron was termed Karegnondi, and also Lake of Orleans. Lake Michigan was called Lake Michigonong, and also Lake of Puans and Illinese, and Lake of the Dauphin. Lake St. Clair was named by La Salle's expedition, from the day on which he entered the river. The length of Lake Superior is estimated at five hundred miles, and its breadth at one hundred and ninety. This lake is as clear as crystal, and the polished stones upon the bottom, as well as numerous shoals of fish, can be seen at a great depth. Lake Michigan is believed to be three hundred and thirty miles long, and sixty miles broad. Lake Huron is two hundred and sixty miles long, and, coastwise, three hundred and sixty; its breadth is one hundred and sixty miles. Lake Erie is two hundred and eighty miles long, and its widest part is about sixty-three miles. Lake St. Clair is thirty miles long and twenty-eight miles broad. It is thus seen that this chain of lakes must furnish an important channel of navigation in the future commerce of the country.

The wild animals of this as well as the other portions of the Northwest are various. The mammoth or mastodon once roamed through its forests, and its skeletons are now found below the surface. Herds of buffaloes roved over the prairies upon the borders of Lake Erie as late as 1720, and we have a full account of that fact from the early French travellers ; but these have been driven, by the progress of emigration, to the plains which sweep along the base of the Rocky Mountains. The elk and moose and troops of deer formerly fed on the green herbage upon the banks of the Detroit ; but these have now retired to the more unsettled portions of the state. The wolverine, the black or brown bear, the wolf, the elk, the deer, moose, lynx, wild-cat, panther, fox, marten, raccoon, porcupine, opossum, weasel, polecat, gopher, the black, red, gray, and striped squirrel, marmot or woodchuck, rabbit, hare, and various other species of animals, are now found in the interior. The beaver, the otter, the muskrat, and the mink inhabit the rivers and small streams, and furnished a valuable article of commerce during the early French, English, and American fur trade. Of birds, the robin, the blackbird, the thrush, the lark, the bluebird, different species of the sparrow, the wren, the woodpecker, the brant, and the loon, the jay, and the cuckoo, are the most common. The forests shelter flocks of the wild turkey and the partridge. The grouse or prairie-hen swarms in the prairies. Pigeons appear in large flocks at particular seasons of the year, and the snipe and the white partridge are not uncommon. The eagle, the brant, the buzzard, and others of the vulture kind, the crow, the raven, the heron, and owls of different species, the most distinguished of which is the great white owl, are among its carnivorous birds. The streams and lakes abound with numerous species of wild ducks, of various and beautiful plumage. They fly in large flocks along the shores of the lakes, and feed in the marshes which fringe them, sometimes blackening the surface by their numbers. The swan may sometimes be seen floating upon the waters; and flocks of wild geese, in the season of summer, collect around the small interior lakes after their winter migrations, where they obtain their food from the wild rice, which is the peculiar product of this region.

The rivers, interior lakes, and surrounding waters of the country abound with fish. These are of various species and of delicious kinds. In the strait of St. Mary and Lake Superior they are of a more valuable sort, from the fact that the water of the latter lake is clear and very cold. The quantity in the last-named lake is very great. The sisquoelle and muckaw, which are not found in other portions of the lake waters, are seen in great abundance in Lake Superior. They sometimes grow to the weight of eight or ten pounds.

The principal fish which are found in the surrounding lakes and interior waters of the country are the sturgeon, whitefish, Mackinaw trout, salmon trout, muskalunjeh, pickerel, pike, perch, herring, the rock bass, the white and black bass, catfish, pout, lamprey eel, bullhead, roach, sunfish, dace, sucker, carp, mullet, billfish, swordfish, bullfish, stone-carrier, sheep's-head, the gar, and many other kinds. The muskalunjeh, Mackinaw trout, and whitefish are deemed most valuable. The former is sometimes caught weighing forty pounds. The Mackinaw trout resembles in lustre and appearance the salmon. The whitefish, a very delicious fish, is similar to the shad, with brighter scales, which appear like burnished silver. This fish has been celebrated by the French travellers from the earliest period, and Charlevoix, who travelled through this region in 1720, once declared that "nothing of the fish kind could excel it." Great numbers of trout and whitefish are taken upon the lakes and shipped to Ohio, New-York, and Pennsylvania, besides those which are consumed in the state.

The nortnern part of the lower peninsula of Michigan, bordering on Lake Huron, has not yet been thoroughly surveyed and brought into market. The soil of this section of the state is not so favourable for agriculture as that of the southern portion. It is more wet and marshy, abounds with pine, and is broken by sandhills and swamps. It has been remarked that the portion of the state bordering on Lake Superior is broken and rocky; and, although containing some elevated table-lands which may be adapted to cultivation, it may be considered unfavourable to agriculture. It has, however, been ascertained to be a rich mineral region. The most settled portion of the state has been organized into counties, as the advance of population has required.

From the brief view which has been taken of the productions of the soil, it is clearly perceived that it affords a variety of resources. The low and densely-wooded land upon the immediate shore of the lower lakes, where the streams run sluggishly over beds of clay, is strikingly contrasted with the more rolling character of the oak lands, extending from this belt towards the centre, dotted as they are by natural ponds of pure water, and coursed by more rapid streams, which have their beds upon sand or gravel; and these in turn are entirely distinct from the more primitive, rocky, and rugged portion lying in that part of the upper peninsula bordering on the shores of Lake Superior. Exhibiting different degrees of fertility, the southern part, from its undulating character and its clear streams, affords a greater inducement for present settlement than the level strip to which allusion has been made, or the more primitive and rocky region of the north. It happens, accordingly, that emigration has in a great measure crossed this strip and sought the more rolling country, leaving the marshes and the mouths of the streams which flow into the eastern side ; a section of the territory which is not only at present unfavourable to settlement from the configuration of the land, but from the fact that it is productive of the class of bilious disorders that prevails in the greater portion of our new country.

CHAPTER II.

First Advance of the Missionaries to the Lakes.—Brebœuf—Daniel—Pijart—Charles Raymbault.—First bark Canoe of white Men reaches St. Mary.—Father Jaques—Bressani—Chaumonotot—Claude Dablon—Mesnard—Lallemand—Gabrielle Dreuillette, and Leonard Gareau.—Réné Mesnard advances to Che-goi-me-gon.—Father Claude Allouez.—Father James Marquette.—Indian Council held at the Falls of St. Mary.—Marquette's Explorations.—His Death.—Robert de la Salle.—His Explorations.—Michilimackinac founded.—Death of La Salle.—Sault de Ste. Marie.—Fort St. Joseph.—Detroit founded.—Its early Condition.—Attacked by the Ottawas.—By the Foxes.—Early French Travellers through the Lakes.

The wide region stretching away in a luxuriant expanse of forest, river, and prairie, from the shores of the great lakes westward to the banks of the Mississippi, was first explored and colonized by the French. That portion of the French territory now comprised in the Canadas, the original point of French settlement, was long the centre of its trade, commerce, and religion ; yet the government claimed the country, both by right of discovery and appropriation, that extended far beyond the boundaries of their actual colonization. Nor were the settlers who had established themselves upon the banks of the St. Lawrence at any time wanting in zeal and enterprise in extending their explorations.

It was early the avowed object of that government to carry the cross of the Catholic Church to the remotest bounds of the Western territory, and thus to secure the advantages of its great resources. The principal directors of the ecclesiastical establishments that were collected at Quebec, found it their policy to become informed of the condition of the domain upon the great lakes ; and as early as 1634, the Jesuits Brebœuf and Daniel joined a party of Hurons who were returning from that walled city, and, passing through the Ottawa River, raised the first hut of the Society of Jesus upon the shore of Lake Iroquois, a bay of Lake Huron, where they daily rang a bell to call the savages to prayer, and performed all those kind offices which were calculated to secure the confidence and affection of the tribes on the lake shores. In order to confirm the missions, a college was founded in Quebec during the following year; and a hospital was established at the same place for the unfortunate of every class, both civilized and savage. Three nuns of Dieppe, in France, were selected to advance into the Canadian wilderness in 1639 ; an Ursuline convent, for the education of girls, was also erected; and at Silleri a small band of the Hurons was trained to the civilization and faith of the French, for the purpose of spreading the religion and influence of their colonies through the Western wilderness.* A plan for the establishment of missions, not only among the Algonquins of the North, but also south of Lake Huron and in Michigan, was formed, indeed, within six years after the discovery of Canada.

The French were at this period excluded from the navigation of Lake Ontario by the hostility of the Mohawks, and their canoes had never ruffled the waters of Lake Erie. The Ottawa, in consequence, was the only avenue to the West; and in 1641 Pijart and Charles Raymbault were found roaming as missionaries among the tribes of Lake Nipissing.

In September, 1641, the first bark canoe, laden with French Jesuits, was paddled through the Ottawa River for the Falls of St. Mary, and, passing by the islands of Lake Huron, they reached these falls after a navigation of seventeen days. At this place they found a large collection of Indians from the neighbouring tribes, many of whom had never seen civilized men, and had never heard of the true God. The white men were invited to dwell among them; for, said the savages, "We will embrace you as brothers; we will derive profit from your words." Raymbault, the first missionary to the tribes of Michigan, feeble with consumption, during the next year returned to Quebec

* Bancroft.

Thus the French at this early period had advanced their missionary posts beyond the shores of Lake Huron and to the outlet of Lake Superior. Father Jaques and Bressani, Jean de Brebœuf, Chaumonotot, Claude Dablon, Mesnard, and others, while carrying the cross through the forests of the North-west, were not to be impeded by tortures and burnings, nor death even, from their darling projects. They toiled and suffered, were struck down with the tomahawk; they lived the life of beggars, and died the death of martyrs; were covered with burning bark, and scalded with boiling water, and scarred with hot iron, until the gentle Lallemand cried out amid his tortures, "We are made a spectacle unto the world, and to angels, and to men:" but with the zeal of ancient martyrdom the Jesuits pressed on from the strongholds of Quebec, filling the ranks of the dead as one after another fell, advancing to the remote boundaries of the lake shores the cross and the lilies of the Bourbons.

During the month of August, 1654, two young fur-traders having joined a band of the Ottawas or Algonquins, in their bark canoes, upon an exploration of five hundred leagues, reappeared after two years before St. Louis with a fleet of fifty canoes. Describing the territory stretching around the great lakes in glowing colours, and the savage hordes which were then scattered through the forests, they sought to effect a wider extension of French commerce into that region. Their request was granted; and in 1656, Gabrielle Dreuillette and Leonard Gareau, former missionaries among the Hurons, were selected for the mission; but just below Montreal a band of Mohawks attacked their fleet, Gareau was mortally wounded, and the expedition prevented. The traders of the lakes, seeking the furs which abounded in those forests, and backed by the Western Indians, who desired a league by which they might resist the Iroquois, soon advanced to Green Bay, and in 1659 two of them passed the winter on the shores of Lake Superior. During the following year they returned to Quebec, escorted by sixty canoes, laden with peltry, and paddled by three hundred Algonquins.

The zeal of Francis de Laval, the bishop of Quebec, appears to have been kindled, by their accounts of the country, with a desire to enter upon the mission, but to Réné Mesnard was allotted this task, so full of hazard. Charged with the duty of exploring the territory around Green Bay and Lake Superior, and of establishing at some convenient point a place for the general assembly of the neighbouring tribes, this aged man, in August, 1660, with but few preparations, departed on his mission, trusting, to use his own words, "in the Providence which feeds the little birds of the desert, and clothes the wild flowers of the forest." During the month of October he reached a bay on the south shore of Lake Superior, which he named St. Theresa; writing to a friend, "in three or four months you may add me to the memento of deaths." After a residence there of eight months, in the year 1661, he complied with the invitation of the Hurons, who had taken refuge in the isle of St. Michael, and, leaving his converts, advanced with one attendant to the Bay of Che-goi-me-gon. Lost in the forest, he was never afterward seen; and among the amulets of the Sioux were discovered his breviary and cassock.*

But the rude missionary posts around the lakes struggled on, and were in danger of falling, when the Canadian colonies were re-enforced in 1665 by a royal regiment, with Tracy as viceroy, Courcelles, a veteran officer, as governor, and Talon, a man of business and perseverance, as intendant, and the representative of the king in civil matters. French enterprise now pressed forward to the West with increased vigour, and in August, 1665 Father Claude Allouez, following the old course of the Ottawa, on the first day of October reached the principal village of the Chippewas in the Bay of Che-goi-me-gon. A chapel dedicated to the Holy Spirit soon arose amid the green luxu-

* Bancroft.

riance of the forest, and the passions of the rough tribes were subdued by paintings which the missionary displayed of the horrors of hell and the terrors of the final judgment. The dwellers around St. Mary flocked to his station; the Hurons and Ottawas, upon the deserts north of Lake Superior, secured his presence at their wigwams; and the Pottowatomies, from the borders of Lake Michigan, invited him to their homes, while the Sacs and Foxes travelled from their villages, and the Illinois came to gather counsel and to describe the beauties of their quiet river. The Sioux, also, from the west of Lake Superior, in a land of prairies, living on wild rice and in skin-covered cabins, welcomed the stranger. After residing for nearly two years upon the southern margin of Lake Superior, in August of 1667 he returned to Quebec, and urged the establishment of permanent missions, to be accompanied by colonies of French emigrants upon the lakes; but in two days after reaching that post, with another priest, Louis Nicholas, he returned to the mission of Che-goi-me-gon.

The condition of Canada at that time was favourable to the progress of the missions of this portion of the West. The monopoly of the West India Company, organized for the purpose of prosecuting the fur-trade, had been yielded up. Peace was enjoyed, and a new recruit of missionaries had arrived from France. Aided by such advantages, Allouez, Claude Dablon, and James Marquette in 1668 repaired to the Chippewas and established the mission of St. Mary, the first settlement commenced by Europeans within the boundaries of Michigan. During the following years these missionaries were employed in strengthening the power of France over the possessions which she claimed, from Green Bay to the head of Lake Superior, and in collecting information respecting the region extending towards the Mississippi. They resolved the following year to attempt its exploration, and selected as a companion a young Illinois, for the purpose of becoming acquainted with the dialect of that tribe.

The commerce of the fur-trade between the Algonquins and the French secured the protection of their tribes and their deep attachment, while a desire of strengthening the power of France over the Western territory pervaded the mind of Louis of France, and Colbert his minister. Talon, the intendant-general, moreover, desired to advance the same object, and for this purpose despatched his agent, Nicholas Perrot, in order to call a general congress of the lake tribes at the Falls of St. Mary. Procuring at Green Bay a guard of Pottowatomies, he reached the settlement of the Miamis at

Chicago, the first of civilized men who had ever visited that point.

The desired Congress of the Indian tribes convened at the Falls of St. Mary in May of 1671, was composed of prominent delegates from the head waters of the St. Lawrence, the Mississippi, the lakes, and even the Red River ; and of veteran officers from the armies of France, intermingled here and there with a Jesuit missionary. A cross having been raised, and also a cedar post marked with the French lilies, the representatives of the savage hordes were informed that they were under the protection of the French king. During that year Marquette gathered a branch of the Hurons at Point St. Ignace, upon the continent north of the peninsula of Michigan, an establishment that was long a convenient resting-place for the savages and the fur-trade.

In 1672, Allouez and Dablon, who were the active agents of the French government in carrying the cross through the eastern part of Wisconsin and the north of Illinois, seeking by mild means to secure the good offices of the Kickapoos upon the Milwaukie and of the Miamis of Lake Michigan, explored the countries to the south of the village that had been thus founded by Marquette, and had even extended their explorations to the tribes of the Foxes, then scattered along the banks of the Fox

River. But the power of the French in this quarter was mainly confined to the immediate shores of the lakes and their connecting waters. Beyond these was a river flowing thousands of miles into the sea, which had never been traced to its outlet, of which Allouez had reported the name to be *Messipi*, or the Great River. This stream, long the object of curious inquiry, was now to be sought, in order that the French power might be spread along its banks.

Thus laboured Marquette, a solitary missionary upon the lakes, until 1673, when M. Talon, the in tendant-general of the colony, ambitious to close his career in that region with something of honour, despatched M. Joliet, a citizen of Quebec, to this man, and unfolded, at the same time, a project for the exploration of the country along the line of the *Michisepee*, or the Great River, to its mouth, which current reports declared flowed into a large sea.* Nor was Marquette unwilling to aid the enterprise. Upon the thirteenth of May, everything being ready, this adventurer, together with Joliet and five other Frenchmen, left Michilimackinac in two bark canoes, supplied with Indian corn and jerked meat, and commenced their voyage to the unknown country. They soon arrived at an Indian village which was familiar to Marquette, and made

* Marquette's Journal.

known to the savages their plan. These savages, however, seemed to be horror-struck at the boldness of the project to explore the great river. There were Indians in that quarter, they told the whites, who would destroy them; monsters who would swallow up them and their canoes; a demon who would ingulf all who ventured near his watery and boiling domain, and heats that would parch them. "I thanked them for their good advice," says Marquette, "but informed them I could not follow it, since the salvation of souls was at stake, for which I should be overjoyed to give my life."

The navigators now passed through Green Bay, from the mud of which there arose, says the voyager, "mischievous vapours, which cause the most grand and perpetual thunders I ever heard." They entered the Fox River, and, dragging their canoes through the rapids, and cutting their feet with the stones, they soon arrived at a village where there lived together a band of the Miamis, Mascoutens, and Kickapoos. Here they found a cross hung with skins, because the Great Spirit had given to the Indians a successful chase. Father Allouez had been here, and had taught them that the cross was the only visible emblem of the true religion. This village was at that time the remote boundary of western exploration, and beyond it no

Frenchman had before gone. They were now journeying through a country before unknown to white men. On the 10th of July the adventurers left these savages amazed at the hardihood of the whites, and, aided by two guides, started for the stream, which was believed to run but three leagues distant from the Mississippi, and to flow into that river. The Indian guides, having conducted them to the portage without any mishap, left them "alone amid that unknown country, in the hand of God." Advancing with prayers, they soon arrived at the Wisconsin, a stream abounding with sand-bars, but studded with islands and bordered by banks green with vegetation, and variegated by groves and pleasant slopes. Floating down the stream in their canoes, they arrived, on the 17th of June, at the Mississippi, "with joy," says Marquette, "that I cannot express."*

The adventurers had now reached the main channel, which they were to explore to its mouth, and, after having admired the herds of buffalo and deer which roamed along its borders, and the swans which floated upon its surface, as well as some great fish which nearly dashed their canoes to atoms, they at length came to the footprints of human beings on the sand, and a trail leading to a

* Early French Travellers in the West, in the North American Review.

meadow. Leaving their canoes in charge of the crew, Joliet and Marquette now advanced towards what seemed to them an Indian village, sufficiently near to hear the voice of the savages. With prayers they made known their presence by a loud cry, and were soon received by an embassy of four old men, who presented them the pipe of peace, and informed them at the same time that they were in a village of the Illinois. The French voyagers were here entertained with a grand feast, accompanied with much smoking. The feast consisted of four courses; the first was of hominy, the second of fish, the third of dog, and the fourth of roasted buffalo. When the feast had been concluded, they were marched through the town with much ceremony, and, having passed the night quietly, they were escorted by six hundred Indians to their canoes. The Illinois, says Marquette, were handsome, kindly, and effeminate. They used guns, and were feared by the savages of the South and West, where they made many prisoners, and sold them as slaves.*

Having left the Illinois, the voyagers passed the rocks on which were painted the monsters of whose existence they had heard at Lake Michigan, and reached the mouth of the Missouri. Leaving the Missouri, they encountered the demon

* Early French Travellers in the West.

against which they had been warned, that was nothing more than a great rock in the stream, and soon arrived at the Ohio. From the Ohio, although somewhat troubled by the moschetoes, they passed in safety to the region of the Arkansas.

At this place they were attacked by a crowd of warriors, and would have been overpowered had not Marquette presented the pipe of peace, which softened the rough savages; for, says the Jesuit, "God touched their hearts." On the succeeding day they proceeded on their way, and were feasted by the hospitable savages upon corn and dogmeat cooked in earthenware, the Indians being amiable and ceremonious, passing the dish from one to another. Here the voyagers determined to return to the North, as they were now confident of the place where the Mississippi was discharged, that being the principal object of the expedition. In consequence, they left Akamsca on the 17th of July, retracing their track; and, amazed at the numbers of "grounds, meadows, woods, buffaloes, stags, deer, wildcats, bustards, swans, ducks, paroquets, and beavers" upon the Illinois River, they arrived at Green Bay in September of that year, where they reported what they had seen.

Father Marquette returned to the Illinois, and performed his clerical offices by their request until the year 1765. On the 18th of May, as he was passing through Lake Michigan in his canoes, he proposed to land at the mouth of a small stream running from the peninsula to perform mass, and retired a little distance to pray. Not returning, his men went in pursuit of him, and soon discovered the missionary, but he was dead; and they made a grave and buried him in the sand, upon the western part of the peninsula of Michigan, on the borders of a stream which now bears his name, and where the place of his interment was recently to be seen. Thus passed away this quiet man in the wilderness, after a long life spent in doing good. Yet he left the impression of his virtues behind him, and his name the world has embalmed and will perpetuate.

At length the enterprise of Robert de la Salle, a native of Normandy, in France, a young man of strong passions but great energy, entered upon a project which had for its object the perpetuation of the power of France by the permanent colonization of the West. La Salle was, according to Charlevoix, brought up among the Jesuits,* and, having lost his patrimony in France, and being of an adventurous and enterprising spirit, he turned his mind to the French colonies on this side of the Atlantic about the year 1670. Having arrived at

* Charlevoix's Letters.

the Canadian port, he occupied himself with a project, popular in that day, connected with a short passage to China, and had already planned an expedition across the great lakes to the banks of the Pacific when Father Marquette returned from the Mississippi. The highly-coloured views which this missionary gave of the country, and its extensive channels of interior communication westward, kindled the sanguine mind of La Salle, and induced him to redouble his exertions to carry out his object. With that view he resorted to M. de Frontenac, then the governor-general of Canada, and at once laid before him the dim but gigantic outline of his project, having for its end the extension of the French power, by constructing a chain of fortifications at the most prominent points along the lakes and rivers of the West. The first step towards this favourite scheme was to rebuild Fort Frontenac, which lies on Lake Ontario, of stone, and the politic adventurer deemed this an important point to win the favour of the governor-general, as that fort was called after his name. Frontenac entered warmly into his views. Believing that the French power would be greatly strengthened by carrying out the design, he advised La Salle to apply directly to the King of France, and, to aid his application for royal patronage, he gave the adventurer letters to Seigneilay, who, as minister of marine, had succeeded his father, the well-known Colbert.

With glowing hopes, La Salle now resorted to the French king, and made known his wants. His plan was approved by the minister, who received his letter, and he was invested with the title of chevalier, and also with the seignory of Fort Frontenac, on the condition that he would rebuild it. From all the nobility of that country he received also assurances of full countenance and aid.* Encouraged by these assurances, La Salle, with his lieutenant, Tonti, an Italian, and thirty men, sailed from Rochelle on the 14th of July, 1678, reached Quebec on the 15th of September of the same year, and soon after proceeded to Fort Frontenac.* Here he found labouring in the missionary cause Louis Hennepin, a friar of the Franciscan order, daring, vain, and determined, ambitious to reap the glory of discovery, and not too scrupulous as to the means. Hennepin had been appointed by his religious superiors acting missionary, to accompany the expedition of La Salle, and arrived at this point, in readiness to meet him, in October of 1678.†

The chevalier having no means to carry out his project, and being at that time somewhat involved

* See Charlevoix's New-France.

† Hennepin's New Discovery.

in debt, was obliged to cast about for money to advance his enterprise. He commenced operations, accordingly, by sending forward a party of his men along the shores of the lakes to collect skins, from which he might accumulate something to pay his winter expenses; for he had an exclusive right from the French monarch to trade in that region. The advantages of this course were twofold: for, while the Frenchmen whom he should despatch were collecting the furs, they could, at the same time, prepare the minds of the Indians for his coming. In the first place, it was made a part of his duty to alter and repair Fort Frontenac; Lake Ontario was to be navigated; a fort was to be built on Lake Erie, and a bark of extraordinary size for those inland seas was to be constructed. All these duties devolved upon himself; and, with the small funds which he had to accomplish them, they would, to a man of moderate soul, have appeared formidable. But to the stout heart of the French cavalier they were as nothing; for his perseverance was unconquerable; and his ambition looked forward to the time when his name should be covered with glory as the benefactor of France, and the Columbus of its colonies in the West.

Having despatched his men for the objects which have been mentioned, La Salle embarked upon Lake Ontario, with his followers, on the 18th of

November, 1678, in a little vessel of ten tons, "the first ship that had ever sailed on that fresh-water sea." Against strong winds the vessel was finally, after having occupied four weeks in beating up from Kingston to Niagara, pushed as near the falls as could be done with safety, and the adventurers landed. Here some magazines were built with great difficulty, as the ground was frozen, and the posts could be driven down only by pouring boiling water upon the surface, and thus thawing the earth. Here also they formed their first acquaintance with the Iroquois of Niagara Village upon Lake Erie, and founded a second fort; but, impeded by the jealousy of the Iroquois, they relinquished the project, and merely erected a temporary work to secure the magazines. Leaving orders for his men to build another vessel, La Salle returned to Fort Frontenac to procure anchors, cables, chains, and other outfits for his new ship. Through the winter days, when Lake Erie lay before them covered with ice, like "a plain paved with fine-polished marble," his men hammered upon the ship, while others gathered furs and peltry in the forest, or strove to gain the good-will of the Iroquois, who claimed the country through which they were to pass, and who had never shown themselves the special friends of the French. On the 20th of January, 1679, the chevalier returned.

The vessel in which his outfits had been embarked was wrecked; and, although the most valuable part of her cargo was saved, the greater portion of her provisions went to the bottom. This, however, did not dishearten the stout-hearted adventurer. A considerable quantity of furs was collected during the winter, with which the commander, in the spring of 1679, returned to Fort Frontenac, and Tonti was sent out upon the shores of the lakes to muster his men, who had been before despatched into that region. The vessel, however, was at length built, in spite of all these obstacles, rigged and manned, and made ready to sail.

The chain of fortifications thus projected by La Salle was afterward constructed upon the water-line of the Northwest, and its remains are still to be seen stretching from the shores of Lake Ontario to the mouth of the Mississippi.

On the seventh day of the month of August, 1679, the bark of sixty tons burden having at length been built, she started on the first voyage which had ever been made upon that inland sea, amid the sound of *Te Deums* and the discharge of arquebuses. This vessel was named the *Griffin*, and the image of that animal was carved on her prow. Robert de la Salle was her commander; and Louis Hennepin, the missionary, burning with ardour to make new discoveries, and also the journalist of the expedition, was on board. The crew consisted of fur-traders taken from the Canadian colonies. They sounded while they ploughed along the waves of Lake Erie, as they did not know the depth of the water, and on the tenth of the same month they arrived near the islands which are grouped at the entrance of the Detroit River, where they anchored.* Hennepin says of these islands, "They make the finest prospect in the world. The strait (of Detroit) is finer than Niagara, being one league broad, excepting that part which forms the lake *that we have called St. Clair.*"

The explorers, passing up the river and advancing across Lake Huron, soon landed on the shore of the northern part of the peninsula of Michigan, and in August they built the old Fort of Michilimackinac. The descriptions of the country by these early travellers, although not entirely accurate, are interesting, and they will be regarded as of great value when the shores of the lakes shall be crowded with a dense population. Of the scenery Hennepin remarks: "The country between the two lakes (Erie and Huron) is very well situated, and the soil very fertile. The banks of the strait (Detroit) are vast meadows, and the prospect is terminated with some hills covered with vineyards, trees bearing good fruit, groves and for-

* Hennepin.

ests so well disposed, that one would think Nature alone could not have made, without the help of art, so charming a prospect. That country is stocked with stags, wild goats, and bears, which are good for food, and not fierce as in other countries ; some think they are better than our pork. Turkey-cocks and swans are there very common ; and our men brought several other beasts and birds, whose names are unknown to us, but they are extraordinary relishing.

"The forests are chiefly made up of walnut, chestnut, plum, and pear trees, loaded with their own fruit, and vines. There is also abundance of timber for building; so that those who shall be so happy as to inhabit that noble country cannot but remember with gratitude them who have led the way."

From Michilimackinac the French explorers went down to Green Bay. Here La Salle collected a cargo of furs, and despatched them in the Griffin back to Niagara, in order to pay the debts which he owed in that quarter. But the vessel was never heard of afterward. With fourteen of his Frenchmen he now paddled down Lake Michigan in canoes, marking the shoals of that lake by bearskins stuck on poles, and feeding on the flesh of that animal. On the first of November, having reached the St. Joseph River of Lake Michigan, he built another rude fort at its mouth, called Fort Miami. Tonti, the Italian, La Salle's lieutenant, had been sent out upon the borders of the lake with some of his men to procure venison and to collect the straggling Frenchmen, and the party remained at St. Joseph awaiting the return of the Griffin.

But winter now came on, and the Griffin did not appear. The party of La Salle, therefore, on the 1st of September, occupied themselves in driving palisades near the mouth of the St. Joseph River of Lake Michigan, in order to warn off the French bark from the shoals upon the borders of that lake. If the lakes should be frozen before the vessel returned, new obstacles would be thrown in his way; for the wilderness presented but few friendly inhabitants and cultivated fields, the shores of the lakes no hospitable ports, so that he determined to proceed upon "his great voyage and glorious undertaking;" and, collecting his crew, and leaving in the rude fort of St. Joseph a few men, he set out with the remainder and three monks. Passing to the Illinois, the party descended that river "by easie journeys, the better to observe that countrey," which abounded with marshes, where no safe footing could be obtained. Through these swamps the adventurers proceeded until they arrived at a village of the Illinois Indians, which contained about five hundred untenanted cabins. Here the party of the Sieur de la Salle, being worn down with hunger, provided themselves with a quantity of corn, which was found hidden in holes in the ground under the Indian wigwams, and placed it on shipboard. This point is supposed to have been the present site of Rock Fort, upon the Illinois.*

On the 4th of January, 1780, the ship being ready and the voyagers prepared, they proceeded into a lake believed to be Peoria, where they caught some good fish with which they might season their corn, when bands of savages appeared on both sides of the river, to which they had now returned. When, however, the startled Frenchmen supposed that, having been engaged in depredation, their season of fighting had arrived, they were agreeably surprised by being asked who they were, the savages "being naturally inclined to peace." The question having been answered, they were received by the Indians with much kindness, who, not as savages are used to do, but "as men well-bred and civilized," spread out before the needy voyagers "beef, and stag, and all sorts of venison and fowls." This hospitable reception was repaid by discharges of firearms, and by presenting them large draughts of brandy. A feast, continuing three days, was at length concluded, and the Frenchmen discovered in the Illinois great humanity, and

* See "Early French Travellers in the West"

a "good disposition to civil society." They were "flatterers complaisant and cunning," and, although they paid a sort of respect to virtue, they were still effeminate and dissolute.* In the midst of this nation La Salle concluded to build another fort, for the pacific character of the Indians in that quarter induced him to select this as its most favourable site. A point upon the rising ground, near the river, was chosen for that object, and here a rude fortification was built, which La Salle named *Crèvecœur*, the Broken Heart: a touching name, indicating his disappointment, occasioned by the loss of the Griffin and the consequent wreck of his hopes, the jealousy of a portion of the savages, who had been persuaded that he was a friend of the Iroquois, and the mutiny of his men, which had already begun to show itself by administering to him poison: misfortunes which sunk him in poverty, casting a gloom over his burning but iron heart, beclouding his glorious visions, and plunging him in doubt and despair.

The winter was passed, and La Salle remained in the wilderness until the vegetation began to spring up on the prairies. Bereft of property, with his men, who even sought his life, fast deserting him, with Indians around him, instigated by capricious and uncertain motives, he still had left his

* Tonti's Account of La Salle's Expedition.

own determined spirit: a spirit fearless of obstacles, which burned the brighter amid the gloom that encompassed it. He found it necessary, therefore, to return to the Canadian colonies to raise men and money, and to prepare another outfit, for he was still firmly resolved to persevere in his original project. In accordance with this determination, he employed M. Dacan and Father Louis Hennepin to proceed from that point on an expedition for the discovery of the sources of the Mississippi, with a party consisting of eight persons, and on the last day of February, 1680, he started them on their voyage. At Fort Crevecœur the chevalier remained until the succeeding November, leaving Tonti and his men among the Illinois, and then departed from that fort for Canada. On his passage along the river, being struck with the position of a high rock upon the bank, he at once determined to construct a fort at that point, and, marking out a plan, sent it to Tonti at Fort Crevecœur. Tonti immediately proceeded to the execution of the project, but had hardly commenced when a revolt broke out among the men whom he had left at Fort Crevecœur, and he was obliged to return. This new fort was named St. Louis, and was placed under the command of Tonti when La Salle returned to France. Its site was probably the spot that is now called Rock Fort, in La Salle county, Illinois.

Tonti, thus left in the woods with a garrison of undisciplined Frenchmen, lived on with little quietude until September of 1681, when, to his horror, a body of the Iroquois appeared in this region, having been irritated during a journey along the borders of the lakes. What was the policy of Tonti in reference to these two hostile savage nations does not clearly appear, yet it is evident that he must have preserved neutral ground, acting as a mediator between them. But succour did not come; and at length he was obliged to return to Canada with five men, in the middle of September of the same year, reaching Lake Michigan in October, and spending the winter upon its borders. Thus ended this expedition for discovery along the shores of the great lakes, under the auspices of an individual who should be known as the first navigator of Lake Erie.

But let La Salle be followed to the close of his adventurous career. He had returned to Canada, where he busied himself in raising recruits, constructing vessels, and gathering funds; and the spring of 1682 found him again upon the Illinois, manning Crevecœur, rebuilding Fort St. Louis, and soon returning to Fort Frontenac to prepare for his second voyage, which commenced on the Illinois River in 1683, when the mouth of the Mississippi was descried. But La Salle soon departed for France, to lay before the throne the record of what he had done, and also his project for the exploration and settlement of the far-famed Louisiana. A fleet was provided by the agency of Seigneilay, consisting of twenty-four vessels, four of which were destined for Louisiana, carrying two hundred and eighty persons, soldiers, artificers, and "women." Starting on his voyage across the ocean, on the 24th of July, 1684, he reached his destined point, where he was assassinated by his own men. Thus fell La Salle; a man of energy, accomplished, virtuous, ardent, and self-sacrificing; one of a class who ruin themselves while they benefit the world, neglect the means of happiness, and raise up for themselves a lasting remembrance.*

No settlement had at this time been made at Detroit, because the traders and Jesuit missionaries had a more direct and safer route to the upper lakes, from Montreal to Michilimackinac, by the way of the Ottawa River. But this point had long been regarded an eligible position for a settlement, as it commanded a broad tract of country, and stood, as it were, at the gate of the upper lakes, in a direct route from these lakes to the English colonies of New-York, by the way of Lake Erie.

The French and English both desired to obtain

* Bancroft.

possession of this post. But while the English were looking to its acquisition, they were anticipated by their rivals. Taking counsel from the movements of their opponents, the French called a grand meeting of the Iroquois, or Five Nations, at Montreal. The chiefs of the different tribes from the St. Lawrence to the Mississippi attended this meeting; also the principal men and the governor-general of Canada. Here the establishment of a post at that place was discussed, and the grounds on which the two nations based their claims to it weighed. The Iroquois, however, said that, understanding the French were about to make a settlement at that point, they were opposed to the measure, as they had already prohibited the English from doing the same. The governor-general of Canada replied that the land belonged neither to the Iroquois nor to the English, but to the King of France, and that there was already an expedition on the march for the purpose of erecting a colonial establishment at that place. In accordance with this plan, Antoine de la Motte Cadillac, lord of Bouaget, Mont Desert, having been granted a tract of fifteen acres square by Louis XIV., left Montreal, accompanied by a Jesuit missionary and one hundred men, and arrived at the point of the wilderness which is now the site of Detroit, in onth of July, 1701, where they commenced the foundation of the first permanent settlement in Michigan.* Before it had only been known by the French missionaries as a trading-post, and in 1620 it was occupied by an Indian village, which was called Teuchsa Grondie.† The Saulte de St. Marie, as we have seen, had at that time been founded, and a rude post was also erected at Fort Gratiot, which was a resting-point for the fur-trade.

This chain of fortifications was all the defence which was constructed upon the lake shores for nearly a century and a half, and it comprised a part of that line of forts that was projected by La Salle, extending from the St. Lawrence down the Mississippi to New-Orleans. Their object was to furnish outposts by which the territory of Canada on the borders of the lakes could be held, the English settlements hemmed in, the Jesuit missionaries and settlers protected against the numerous and capricious tribes of savages in this quarter, and by which the fur-trade might circulate, with full success, along the lakes and streams of the North-west. The forts of Detroit, Michilimackinac, St. Joseph, and Green Bay were of rude construction, and the chapels erected by their side were used for the religious assemblies of the French settlers, who were from that time collected around the

* Charlevoix. † Colden.

posts, and also of the Indians who were under the special guardianship of the Jesuit missionaries. These structures, minute points on the borders of the forest, were either roofed with bark or thatched with straw, and on their top was generally erected the cross. Tribes of friendly Indians that could be induced to settle near them, had their villages or wigwams around these posts, and also their planting-grounds, in which they cultivated Indian corn, not only for the French settlers, but also for the persons connected with the fur-trade.* They derive their principal importance from the fact that they were the only outposts of the French government in this country before the English conquest, and, consequently, the theatres of the most interesting frontier operations.

About three years after Detroit was founded, the Ottawa Indians in that vicinity were invited to Albany, in New-York, upon what was supposed to be a friendly visit. As St. Joseph was surrounded by villages of the Hurons, Pottawatomies, and Miamis, so also was Detroit at that time guarded by parts of the friendly tribes of the Hurons and Pottawatomies near the settlements, and an Ottawa village had been erected on the opposite bank of the river. It would appear that while the Ottawas were in Albany, they had been persuaded by the

* La Hontan's Voyages.

English, who even then wished to obtain possession of the post of their rivals, that it was the design of the French to wrest the dominion of the country from their hands; and they accordingly set fire to the town, but without success, as the fire was soon extinguished. At this time, also, groups of savages of the same tribe, having made a successful expedition against their enemies the Iroquois, and warm with victory, were seen paraded in hostile array in front of the fort; but M. Tonti, who was the commandant of the post, despatching the Sieur de Vincennes against them, he dispersed their bands, and rescued the Iroquois prisoners whom they left behind them in their flight.*

The progress of operations on the lake shores was not at this period marked with any very great interest, as the settlements were few; but they reflect, nevertheless, the spirit which prevailed in France during their continuance. The lands lay sleeping in their original silence and solitude, undisturbed by the plough. Occasionally the settlers may have been surprised by their ancient enemies the Iroquois, but the appearance of parts of these nations excited a surprise which soon settled down into peace. But in 1712, the Ottagamies or Foxes, who had been before but little known, but who were probably in secret alliance with the Iroquois,

* Cass.

projected a plan for the destruction of Detroit. They made their arrangements in secret, and sent their bands to collect around the new French settlement, which was then garrisoned by a force of twenty soldiers, of whom M. Du Buisson was the commandant. The occupants of the three French villages of Indians, the Ottawas, Pottawatomies, and Hurons, were then absent on a hunting excursion. A converted Indian, however, under the influence of a Jesuit missionary, disclosed their plot before it was ripe for execution, and Du Buisson immediately sent despatches through the forest to call in the aid of the friendly Indians, and prepared for an effective defence.

On the 13th of May of that year, the Foxes made their onset upon Detroit with fiendish yells. No sooner, however, was the attack commenced, than portions of the friendly Indians were seen through the wilderness, painted for battle as is their custom, and the gates of the fort were opened to receive them. A consultation was now held at the council-house, and they renewed their league with Du Buisson, and expressed their determination, if necessary, to die in the defence of the post. On the arrival of the friendly Indians, the Foxes retreated to the forest which now adjoins the eastern boundary of Detroit, and intrenched themselves in their camp.

The French then sallied out from the fort, and, backed by their savage allies, erected a blockhouse in front of their camp, in order to force the enemy from their position. Here the latter were closely besieged; being cut off from their supply of water, and driven to desperation by thirst and famine, they in turn rushed out from their strongholds upon the French and the friendly Indians, and succeeded in getting possession of a house near the village. This house they fortified, but they were here attacked by the French cannon, and driven back to their former intrenchment.

Finding that their league was likely to prove unsuccessful, the Foxes now sent despatches to the French commandant, asking for peace, which was denied them. Upon this they considered themselves insulted, and, burning with revenge, they discharged showers of blazing arrows upon the fort. The lighted matches they had affixed to their arrows coming in contact with the dry roofs of the houses, kindled them into flame, when the precaution was taken to cover the rest with wet skins, and by this means they were preserved.* The desperation of the Foxes almost discouraged the French commandant, and he had nearly determined to evacuate Detroit and to retire to Michilimackinac, when his Indian allies promised to re-

* Cass.

double their efforts for his defence; and the war-songs and dances of their bands, heard through the solitude of the forest, assured him that a more desperate effort was about to be made in his behalf. The preparations having been finished, the French and Indians advanced upon the Foxes with more determined courage, and, pouring upon their intrenchments a deadly fire, they were soon filled with the dying and the dead. Once more the Foxes demanded peace. Before any capitulation, however, was completed, the enemy retreated towards Lake St. Clair during a storm at midnight, on the nineteenth day of the siege.*

The French and their Indian allies, as soon as they discovered their flight, prepared for a pursuit, and soon came upon their camps. An action began, which at the outset was in favour of the Foxes, the French and Indians being repulsed. But a different plan of operation was soon after adopted, and with better success. At the end of three days a field-battery was completed, and the intrenchment of the Foxes fell before the French cannon.

The Foxes may be considered the Ishmaelites of the wilderness, for they were at enmity with all the tribes on the lakes. They collected their forces on the Fox River of Green Bay, where they

* Cass.

commanded the territory between the lakes and the Mississippi, so that it was dangerous for travellers to pass through that region except in large bodies, and armed, while their warriors were sent out to seek objects of plunder and devastation. So great was the danger apprehended by the missionaries and traders in passing through that territory, as well as by the French settlers, and so great the injury already done by those tribes, that an expedition was fitted out against them by the French, backed by their Indian allies, who were rankling under a sense of repeated wrongs. This warlike nation had stationed itself on the banks of the Fox River, at a place then and now called by the French *Butte des Morts*, or the Hill of the Dead, defending their position by a ditch and three courses of palisades.* Here they collected their women and children, and prepared for a desperate resistance. M. de Louvigny, the commandant of the expedition, perceiving the strength of their works, determined not to expose his men by a direct attack, but entered upon a regular siege, and was preparing for the final crisis when the Foxes proposed a capitulation. This was accepted ; and the pride of the Foxes being thus humbled, they sank into obscurity during the remainder of the French war.*

* Cass.

Thus it is seen that, although the few French forts upon the lakes were rudely constructed, and but poorly adapted to make a serious and effective defence, they were nevertheless competent, with their small garrisons, to protect the emigrants against the disaffected tribes which were from time to time arrayed against them. The pickets which surrounded them, composed of upright stakes, furnished a line of concealment rather than strong bulwarks, and, together with the light cannon with which they were mounted, enabled the French to suppress the disturbances that occasionally sprang up around their posts.*

The early missionaries and French travellers who journeyed through the region of the lakes exhibit a peculiar form of character. Tinctured with the spirit which prevailed in France at the period of their immigration, the novel scenes around them impressed them with those sentiments of romance so peculiar to the French. They show the spirit under which the missionaries and soldiers travelled, and the eloquence with which the scenes around them tended to inspire their minds.

The forests amid which their lot was cast were calculated to fill them with wonder and admiration. A vast chain of inland seas, which appeared to them like oceans, stretched a watery horizon

* Cass.

along the borders of the wilderness. Flocks of water-fowl of varied plumage streamed along the shores of the lakes, and the waters swarmed with fish. The face of nature, fresh in the luxuriance of a virgin soil, was everywhere clothed with magnificent vegetation. Did they travel through the Indian trails or bridle-paths which wound through the forest, extensive tracts of oaklands, that seemed like cultivated parks, met their eye, studded with little crystal lakes and streams, and covered with flowers. Herds of buffaloes wandered over the prairies, trampling down the flowers which blushed in their track as they rushed on in clumsy motion.* Great numbers of moose and elk, which in the size of their horns almost rivalled the branches of the trees, bounded through the thickets. Deer were here and there seen feeding upon the margin of the water-courses. Flocks of wild turkeys and other game filled the woods; the prairies were alive with grouse, and pigeons swept along like clouds above the forest, in numbers which sometimes almost hid the sun.

But more than this, they beheld in the luxuriance of the soil a prize which, if judiciously managed, would be a source of inexhaustible wealth to their nation. Rich clusters of grapes hung from the trees, which reminded them of the champaign dis-

* Charlevoix.

tricts of France from which they emigrated; and apples and plums, crude to the taste, but that by culture might be much improved, abounded in the groves.

"Lake Erie," says La Hontan, who commanded a fort upon it in 1688, "is justly dignified with the illustrious name of Conti; for assuredly it is the *finest* upon earth. You *may* judge of the goodness of the climate from the latitude of the countries that surround it. Its circumference extends to two hundred and thirty leagues, but it affords everywhere a charming prospect, and its shores are decked with oak-trees, elms, chestnut-trees, walnut, apple, plum-trees, and vines which bear their fine clusters up to the very tops of the trees, upon a sort of ground that lies as smooth as one's hand. Such ornaments as these are sufficient to give rise to the most agreeable idea of a landscape in the world. I cannot express what quantities of deer and turkeys are to be found in these woods, and in the vast meadows that lie upon the south side of the lake. At the foot of the lake we find wild beeves (buffaloes), upon the banks of two pleasant streams that disembogue into it, without cataracts or rapid currents. It abounds with sturgeon and whitefish, but trouts are very scarce in it, as well as the other fish that we take in the Lakes of Hurons (Huron) and Illinese (Michigan). It is clear of shelves, rocks, and banks of sand, and has fourteen or fifteen fathoms water. The savages assure us that it is never disturbed by high winds except in the months of December, January, and February, and even then but seldom, which I am very apt to believe, for we had very few storms when I wintered in my fort in 1688, though the fort lay open to the Lake of Hurons. The banks of this lake are commonly frequented by none but warriors, whether the Iroquese, the Illinese, the Oumamiés, &c., and it is very dangerous to stop there. By this means it comes to pass that the stags, roebucks, and turkeys run in great bodies up and down the shore all around the lake. In former times the Errironons and the Andastogueronons lived upon the confines of the lake; but they were extirpated by the Iroquese, as well as the other nations marked on the map."*

Charlevoix, who travelled through the region of the lakes in 1720 as an accredited agent of the French government, gives an account equally interesting respecting the condition of the country at the time when he wrote. "The first of June being the day of Pentecost," says he, "after having travelled up a beautiful river for the space of an hour, which has its rise, as they say, at a great

* La Hontan's Voyages.

distance, and runs between two fine meadows, we passed over a carrying-place of about sixty paces in breadth, in order to avoid turning round a point which is called the Long Point. It is a very sandy spot of ground, and naturally bears a great quantity of vines. The following days I saw nothing remarkable, but coasted along a charming country, hid at times by very disagreeable prospects, which, however, are of no great extent. Wherever I went ashore, I was enchanted by the beauty and variety of a prospect which was terminated by the noblest forests in the whole world. Add to this, that every part of it swarms with water-fowl. I cannot say whether the woods afford game in equal profusion, but I well know that on the south side there is a prodigious quantity of buffaloes. Were we all to sail as I then did, with a serene sky, in a most charming climate, and in water as clear as that of the purest fountain ; were we sure of finding everywhere secure and agreeable places to pass the night in, where we might enjoy the pleasure of hunting at a small expense, breathe at our ease the purest air, and enjoy the prospect of the finest countries in the universe, we might possibly be tempted to travel to the end of our days. I recalled to mind those ancient patriarchs who had no fixed place of abode ; who lived in tents ; who were, in a manner, the masters of all the countries they passed through; and who enjoyed in peace and tranquillity all their productions, without the plague inevitable in the possession of a real and fixed estate. How many oaks represented to me that of Mamre! How many fountains put me in mind of that of Jacob! Each day a new situation, chosen at pleasure; a neat and commodious house, built and furnished with all necessaries in less than a quarter of an hour, and floored with a pavement of flowers continually springing up on a carpet of the most beautiful green; on all sides simple and natural beauties, unadulterated and inimitable by any art."*

Charlevoix at that early period visited Detroit for the purpose of viewing the young colony, where he recommended that an accession should be made to the strength of the infant settlement from Montreal. This addition to their power was approved of by the French, on the ground that it would secure them the fur-trade, then too much within reach of the English of New-York. He also attended, while here, a council of the chiefs of the three villages near Detroit, where the question was discussed whether it was proper to introduce brandy among the Indians, a practice which the Jesuits finally succeeded in abolishing. In alluding to Detroit, he says, "It is pretended that this is the

* Charlevoix's Journal.

finest part of all Canada; and really, if we can judge by appearances, nature seems to have denied it nothing which can contribute to make a country delightful: hills, meadows, fields, lofty forests, rivulets, fountains, rivers, and all of them so excellent in their kind, and so happily blended as to equal the most romantic wishes. The lands, however, are not equally proper for every kind of grain; but most are of a wonderful fertility, and I have known some produce good wheat for eighteen years running without any manure; and, besides, all of them are proper for some particular use. The islands seem placed on purpose for the pleasure of the prospect, the river and lake abound in fish, the air is pure, and the climate temperate and extremely wholesome."* †

* Charlevoix's Journal.

† These travellers were not, nor could they be expected to be in all cases accurate, from their rapid passage through the Western territory; but in their accounts of their own experience we derive much valuable information of its actual condition during the time when they wrote. Glimpses of wild beasts which they had never before seen, vegetable productions whose names they did not know, fragments of facts collected from the accounts of the Indians, always exaggerated and seldom authentic, passed in rapid succession before their minds, while they journeyed onward in bewildered amazement, through rivers, lakes, forests, and Indian camps; and their impressions, thus coloured and distorted, found their way into their books. But, taken as a whole, their accounts are as accurate as could be expected, considering the circumstances under which they wrote.

The Jesuit being requested by Tonti to visit the great council at Detroit, consented to do so on the day of his arrival; and his account of that council is here transcribed

"On the 7th of June, which was the day of my arrival at the fort (Detroit), Mons. de Tonti, who commands here, assembled the chiefs of the three villages I have just mentioned, in order to communicate to them the orders he had received from the Marquis de Vaudreuil. They heard him calmly and without interruption. When he had done speaking, the orator of the Hurons told him in a few words that they were going to consult about what he had proposed to them, and would give him their answer in a short time. It is the custom of the Indians not to give an immediate answer on an affair of any importance. Two days afterward they assembled at the commandant's, who was desirous I should be present at this council, together

If, for example, the zealous Marquette depicts "wingless swans" as floating upon the Mississippi; if Hennepin describes "wild goats" upon the shores of Lake Erie; if La Hontan discourses upon the "Long River," and Charlevoix alludes to the "citrons" as growing upon the banks of the Detroit, we are disposed to attribute their inaccuracies less to intentional misrepresentation than to natural and obvious mistake. Accurate observation and minute care are required to establish with perfect correctness the facts connected with any country, and he who should look to early records for historical matter will find much chaff to be winnowed from the genuine and golden wheat.

with the officers of the garrison. Sasteratfi, whom the French call King of the Hurons, and who is, in fact, hereditary chief of the Tionnontatez, who are the true Hurons, was also present on this occasion; but as he is still a minor, he came only for form's sake: his uncle, who governs in his name, and who is called regent, spoke in quality of orator of the nation. Now the honour of speaking in the name of the whole is generally given to some Huron, when any of them happen to be of the council. The first view of their assemblies gives you no great idea of the body. Imagine to yourself, madame, half a score of savages almost stark naked, with their hair disposed in as many different manners as there are persons in the assembly, and all of them equally ridiculous; some with laced hats, all with pipes in their mouths, and with the most unthinking faces. It is, besides, a rare thing to hear one utter so much as a single word in a quarter of an hour, or to hear any answer made even in monosyllables; not the least mark of distinction, nor any respect paid to any person whatsoever. We should, however, be apt to change our opinions of them on hearing the result of their deliberations."*

This, as is described by Charlevoix, was the general mode in which the Indian councils were

* Charlevoix's Journal.

neld with the French upon the lakes when questions of importance were to be decided. It was necessary to secure the concurrence of the savages in every measure of policy, so that these tribes should co-operate with them in carrying it into effect.

CHAPTER III.

Colonial Emigrants.—Merchants.—Coureurs des Bois.—The Peasantry.—French Soldiers.—Legal Administration.—Policy of the French Government.—Indian Mythology of the Lakes.—Mode of Land Distribution.—Increase of Colonization.—The Fur-trade of the Lakes.—Canadian Boat-songs.—La Hontan's Account of the Fur-trade.

THE posts of the French upon the lakes, while the Western territory was under their government, exhibit a peculiar form of character, combined with institutions no less singular. The few feeble colonies that were scattered through this territory had emigrated principally from Brittany and Normandy, provinces of France. Working men, drawn from the more dense settlements around Quebec and Montreal, the seats of the bishops, the seigneurs, and the Jesuits, they were sent out for the purpose of building up the posts, and of protecting the fur-trade carried on through the chain of the great lakes. Despatched for these objects, they were expected to endure cheerfully the hardships they would be called on to encounter in their establishment. The population assembled at these posts consisted of the military by which they were garrisoned, Jesuits, priests, merchants, traders, and peasants. But a small portion of this population, however, was stationary. It was moved from place to place, as the interests of the French government seemed to require.

The French commandants at these posts were, the most prominent individuals, and, with their garrisons, constituted a little monarchy within themselves. Their power was arbitrary, extending to the right of doing whatever they might deem expedient for the welfare of the settlements, whether in making laws or in punishing crimes. Under this simple and imperfect form of government, the oldest merchants residing at the several posts were reverenced as the head men of their particular colony. Careful and frugal in their habits, without much of what we should call rigid virtue, it was their policy to exercise their influence among the settlers with paternal mildness, that they might secure their obedience, to keep on good terms with the Indians in order to retain their trade, and they often fostered a large number of half-breed children around their posts, who were the offspring of their licentiousness.

The *Coureurs des Bois*, or rangers of the woods, were either French or half-breeds, a hardy race, accustomed to labour and privation, and thoroughly conversant with the character and habits of the

* La Hontan's Voyages.

savage tribes from which they obtained their furs and peltry. They could, with no less skill than the Indians, ply the oar of the light canoe upon the waters of the lakes, were equally dexterous in hunting and trapping, and, as they pointed their rifles at the squirrel on the top of the tallest tree, they could confidently say to their ball, like the ancient warrior, "to the right eye." These half-breeds generally spoke the language both of their French and Indian parents, and knew just enough of their religion to be alike regardless of that of each. Employed by the French companies as voyageurs or guides, their forms, which were models of manly beauty, were developed to great strength by propelling the canoe along the lakes and rivers, and by carrying heavy packs of merchandise for the fur-trade across the portages, by means of leather straps, suspended from their shoulders or resting against their foreheads. From having travelled through numerous points of the wilderness, they became familiar with the trails of the most remote Indian tribes, and with the depth of the water in every inlet and stream of the lakes, as well as with every island, rock, and shoal. Their ordinary dress was a "moleton" or blanket-coat, a red cap, a belt of cloth passed around the middle, and a loose shirt.* Sometimes, in their voyages through

* Henry.

the lakes, they wore a brown coat or cloak, with a cape which could be drawn up from their shoulders over their heads like a hood. At other times they had on elkskin trowsers, the seams of which were ornamented with fringes, a surtout of coarse blue cloth reaching to the calf of the leg, a scarlet-coloured worsted sash fastened about the waist, in which was stuck a broad knife employed in dissecting the animals taken in hunting, and moccasins made of buckskin. Affable, gay, and active, these men were employed by the French merchants either as guides, canoemen, carriers, or traders, to advance into the wilderness and procure their furs from the Indians, to transport them along the lakes and streams, and lodge them in the several depôts or factories which were established in connexion with the French forts.

The peasants, or that class of the lake settlers who cultivated small patches of ground within the narrow circle of their picket-fences, were few. Their dress was peculiar, and even wild. They wore surtouts of coarse blue cloth, fastened at the middle with a red sash, a scarlet woollen cap containing a scalping-knife, and moccasins made of deerskin. Civilization and barbarism were here strangely mingled. Groups of Indians from the remotest shores of the lakes, wild in their garb, would occasionally make their appearance at the settlements with numerous canoes laden with beaver-skins, which they had brought down to these places of deposite. Among them were intermixed the French soldiers of the garrison, with their blue coats turned up with white facings,* and the Jesuits, with their long gowns and black bands, from which were suspended by silver chains the rosary and crucifix, who, with the priests, had their stations around the forts, and ministered in the chapels.

Agriculture was but little encouraged by the policy of the fur-trade or the character of the population. It was confined to a few patches of Indian corn and wheat, which they rudely cultivated, with little knowledge of correct husbandry. They ground their grain in windmills, which were scattered along the banks of Detroit River and the St. Clair lake. The recreations of the French colonists consisted in attending the religious services held in the rude chapels on the borders of the wilderness, in adorning their altars with wild flowers, in dancing to the sound of the violin at each other's houses, in hunting the deer through the oak-land openings, and in paddling their light canoes across the clear and silent streams. The women employed themselves in making coarse cotton and woollen cloths for the Indian trade. In

* Manuscript Journals from Detroit.

their cottages were hung rude pictures of saints, the Madonna and child, and the leaden crucifix supplied the place of one of silver. Abundance of game strayed in the woods, and the waters were alive with fish.

As these immigrants were sent out by the French government, they were provided by its direction, through the commissariat department, with canvass for tents, hoes, axes, sickles, guns, so many pounds of powder, and meat, with the stipulation that these should be paid for when a certain quantity of land had been cleared.*

The Jesuits, who were the most active agents in the exploration of these regions, were, as a class, persons of highly-cultivated and intelligent minds, and of polished manners. The narratives of their wanderings through the wilderness throw a colouring of romance around the prairies, and forests, and lakes, which amounts almost to a classic spirit; yet they have left upon the lake-shores but few monuments either of their benevolence or their enterprise. The success of the Jesuits among the Indians was small compared with the extent of their labours. By the savages these Catholic missionaries were regarded as medicine-men and jugglers, on whom the destiny of life and death depended; and, although they were greatly feared,

* Manuscript Journals from Detroit.

they succeeded in making but few converts to their religious faith, excepting young children, or Indians just about to sink into their graves.

The administration of the law around these scattered posts was founded on no compact and settled system. The *Coutume de Paris*,* or custom of Paris, was the law of Canada; but this code, although it was received and practised upon in the older and more populous settlements of the lower province, was not adopted and enforced with any degree of uniformity or strictness among the more distant colonists. The commandants of the posts had the principal cognizance of the population around them, and exercised their authority in a mild, though arbitrary manner. Indeed, such was the feudal character of this law, that the French paid a willing and implicit obedience to their commandants, who, being invested with unlimited power, were styled the "governors of the posts." A perfect system of law can exist only where there is sufficient intelligence to mark out and determine the rule of right, and sufficient moral power to enforce it. A register was kept, in which the character and circumstances of the colonists were recorded, and in which the Jesuit or the commandant of the post might inspect the condition of each one as upon a map. There was

* See the *Coutume de Paris*, in three volumes.

here no system of education like that which prevailed in New-England; and all the knowledge acquired by the children of the colonists was obtained from the priests, and related to the tenets of the Catholic Church.*

A singular form of character was also thrown around the territory by the mythology of the savages. The Indians had not only their good *Manitos*, but their evil spirits; and the wild features of the lake scenery appears to have impressed their savage minds with superstition. They believed that all the prominent points of this wide region were created and guarded by monsters; and the images of these they sculptured on stone, painted upon the rocks, or carved upon the trees. Those who obeyed these supernatural beings, they thought, would after death range among flowery fields filled with the choicest game, while those who neglected their counsels would wander amid dreary solitudes, stung by "gnats as large as pigeons."†

The plan of distributing the land was calculated to prevent the settlement of the country. A law was passed requiring the houses of the inhabitants to be placed upon ground with a front of only one acre and a half, and running forty acres back.‡

* Manuscript Journals. † Henry.
‡ See Appendix A, B.

This kept the settlements in a close line along the banks of the streams. A feudal and aristocratic spirit also controlled the grants of land. The commandants of the forts had the power to convey lands, with the permission of the governor-general of Canada, subject to the confirmation of the King of France, the right of shooting hares, rabbits, and partridges being reserved to the grantor. The grantee was bound to clear and improve the land within three years from the date of his deed. The timber that might be necessary for the construction of fortifications or vessels was reserved; and no person was permitted to work upon his land at the trade of a blacksmith, gunsmith, armorer, or brewer, but on pain of forfeiture. He was forbidden the trafficking in spirituous liquors with the Indians; and, what was the most singular requisition of all, he was bound to plant or assist in planting a long Maypole at the door of the principal manor on the first of May in each year. Such were the feudal features of this system, equally opposed to the increase of the settlements, to freedom, and independence. How striking is the contrast between this system and the policy of our American laws now acting on the soil, which, by furnishing land cheap, offer every encouragement to agriculture, and thus freely open the treasures of the earth to the labours of our hardy and enterprising citizens.

As early as 1749, the post of Detroit and the others upon the Northwestern lakes, Michilimackinac, Ste. Marie, and St. Joseph, received an accession of immigrants. The last two were called after the saints of those names in the Catholic calendar. Michilimackinac derives its name from the Indian words *Michi-mackinac*, meaning a great turtle, from its supposed resemblance to that animal, or from the Chippewa words *Michine-maukinonk*, signifying the place of giant fairies, who were supposed by Indian superstition to hover over the waters around that beautiful island.* The origin of the name of Detroit is the French word *Detroit*, signifying a strait, because the post was situated on the strait connecting Lake Erie with Lake St. Clair.

During the whole period of the French domination, extending from the first settlement of the country down to the year 1760, the traffic of Michigan was confined principally to the trade in furs. This interesting traffic upon the great lakes was carried on by the French under peculiar circumstances. As the forests of the lake region abounded with furs which were of great value in the mother-country, it became an important object with the Canadian government to prosecute that trade with all the energy in its power. The rich

* Schoolcraft's Algic Researches.

furs of the beaver and otter were particularly valuable, from the great demand for them in Europe. Large canoes made of bark, and strongly constructed, were despatched annually to the lakes, laden with packs of European merchandise, consisting of blankets, printed calicoes, ribands, cutlery, and trinkets of various kinds, which the Indians used, and Detroit, Michilimackinac, and Ste. Marie were their principal places of deposite.

To secure the interests of the large companies, licenses for this trade were granted by the governor-general of Canada to the merchants, who sometimes sold them to the coureurs des bois. The possessor of one of these licenses was entitled to load two large canoes, each of which was manned by six men. The cargo of one of these canoes was valued at about a thousand crowns. This merchandise was sold to the traders on a credit, and at about fifteen per cent. advance on the price it would command in ready money. But the voyages were very profitable, and there was generally a gain of about one hundred per cent. on the sum invested in the enterprise. The traders endured most of the fatigue, and the merchants received most of the profit. On the return of one of these expeditions, six hundred crowns were taken by the merchant for his license; and as he had sold the thousand crowns' worth of goods at their prime cost, from this sum he also deducted forty per cent. for bottomry; the remainder was then divided among the six coureurs des bois, who were thus left with but a small compensation for all their perils and hardship.*

The *coureurs des bois* were the active agents of the fur-trade. Thoroughly acquainted with the navigation of the lakes, they fearlessly swept along the waters of these inland seas, encamping at night upon its shores. Of mixed white and Indian blood, they formed the connecting link between civilization and barbarism. Their dress was also demi-savage. Lively and sanguine, they were at all times ready to join the Indians in the dance, or pay respect to their ceremonies. Their French fathers had familiarly associated with the native tribes, and their mothers and wives were the inmates of Indian camps. In many respects their character resembled that of mariners upon the ocean, for the same general causes might be said to operate upon both. Instead of navigating the high seas in ships tossed by storms, and ploughing the waves from port to port, it was their lot to propel their light canoes over the fresh-water seas of the forest; where, hurried from one Indian village to another, like the mariner on the ocean,

* La Hontan's Voyages.

they acquired all those habits which belong to an unsettled and wandering life.

Advancing to the remote shores of Lake Superior or Lake Michigan, and following the courses of the rivers which flow into them, as soon as they reached the points where the Indians were in the habit of resorting, they at once encamped. Here they opened their packages of goods, exhibited them to their savage customers, and exchanged them for furs; and, having disposed of all their merchandise, and loaded their canoes with the peltries it had procured, they bade adieu to their Indian friends, and started on their voyage back, with feathers stuck in their hats, keeping time with their paddles to the Canadian boat-song.*

La Hontan, in his Journal, which was published in France, and a translation of which was afterward published in this country, gives an interesting account of the fur-trade, showing the general course of that traffic while the Canadas were under the French. The author resided at Montreal. At this time (1688) Michilimackinac was the principal stopping-place for the traders on their way from Montreal or Detroit to the forests bordering on Lake Superior. Here their goods were deposited, and here the furs were collected for their return freight. Sometimes, however, the traders,

* Tales of the Northwest.

accompanied by numerous canoes of the Ottawas, would proceed directly to the older settlements on the St. Lawrence, where they supposed they might be able to dispose of their cargoes to greater advantage than at the interior posts.

The following is La Hontan's account of the fur-trade at the period referred to :

"Much about the same day," says he, "there arrived twenty-five or thirty canoes, being homeward bound from the great lakes, and laden with beaver-skins. The cargo of each canoe amounted to forty packs, each of which weighs fifty pounds, and will fetch fifty crowns at the farmer's office. These canoes were followed by fifty more of the Ottawas and Hurons, who come down every year to the colony in order to make a better market than they can do in their own country of Michilimackinac, which lies on the banks of the Lake of Hurons, at the mouth of the Lake of Illinese (Michigan). Their way of trading is as follows :

"Upon their arrival they encamp at the distance of five or six hundred paces from the town. The first day is spent in ranging their canoes, unloading their goods, and pitching their tents, which are made of birch bark. The next day they demand audience of the governor-general, which is granted them that same day, in a public place.

"Upon this occasion each nation makes a ring

for itself. The savages sit upon the ground with pipes in their mouths, and the governor is seated in an arm-chair; after which there starts up an orator or speaker from one of these nations, who makes an harangue importing that his brethren are come to visit the governor-general, to renew with him their wonted friendship; that their chief view is to promote the interest of the French, some of whom, being unacquainted with the way of traffic, and being too weak for the transporting of goods from the lakes, would be unable to deal in beaver-skins if his brethren did not come in person to deal with them in their own colonies. That they knew very well how acceptable their arrival is to the inhabitants of Montreal, in regard of the advantage they reap from it; that, in regard to the beaver-skins, they were much valued in France, and the French goods given in exchange were of an inconsiderable value; and that they mean to give the French sufficient proof of their readiness to furnish them with what they desire so earnestly.

"That, by way of preparation for another year's cargo, they are come to take in exchange fusees, and powder and ball, in order to hunt great numbers of beavers, or to gall the Iroquese in case they offered to disturb the French settlements; and, in fine, in confirmation of their words, that they throw a porcelain collar (belt of wampum), with some beaver-skins, to the kitchi-okima (so they call the governor-general), whose protection they laid claim to in case of any robbery or abuse committed upon them in the town. The spokesman having made an end of his speech, returns to his place and takes up his pipe, and the interpreter explains the substance of the harangue to the governor, who commonly gives a very civil answer, especially if the presents be valuable, in consideration of which he likewise makes them a present of some trifling things. This done, the savages rise up and return to their huts, to make suitable preparation for the ensuing truck.

"The next day the savages make their slaves carry the skins to the houses of the merchants, who bargain with them for such clothes as they want. All the inhabitants of Montreal are allowed to traffic with them in any commodity but rum and brandy, these two being excepted upon the account that when the savages have got what they want, and have any skins left, they drink to excess, and then kill their slaves; for when they are in drink they quarrel and fight, and if they were not held by those who are sober, would certainly make havoc one of another. However, you must observe that none of them will touch either gold or silver. As soon as the savages have made an end of their truck, they take leave of the governor, and so return home by the *River Ottawas*. To conclude, they do a great deal of good, both to the poor and rich, for you will readily apprehend that everybody turns merchant upon such occasions."*

To the question what was the condition of the Northwest Territory when it was claimed and occupied by France, we can furnish a ready answer. It was a vast ranging-ground for the numerous Indian tribes, who roamed over it in all the listless indolence of their savage independence; of the Jesuit missionaries, who, under the garb of their religious orders, strove to gain the influence of the red men in behalf of their government as well as their Church, by their conversion to the Catholic faith; the theatre of the most important military operations of the French soldiers at the West; and the grand mart where the furs, which were deemed the most valuable products of this region, were collected for shipment to France, under a commercial system which was originally projected by the Cardinal de Richelieu.

The condition of a country, although often in some measure modified by the nature of the climate and the soil, is more generally founded upon the character of the people and that of its laws. This is clearly exhibited in the case of the North-

* La Hontan's Voyages.

west; for while that domain was rich in all the natural advantages that could be furnished by the soil, it was entirely barren of all those moral and intellectual fruits springing from bold and energetic character, directed by a free, enlightened, and wholesome system of jurisprudence.

CHAPTER IV.

Struggle between France and England for the Possession of the Country.—The Iroquois and Algonquins.—British Troops advance into Canada.—Battle of Quebec.—Death of Wolfe and Montcalm.—British Detachment under Rogers takes Possession of Michigan.—Rogers traverses Lake Erie.—Pontiac makes his first Appearance.—Bellestre.—Surrender of Detroit.

WHILE the forests were thus reposing in the silence of nature, broken only by the peaceful operations of the fur-trade, more important events were transpiring beyond their eastern boundary. From the Atlantic to Quebec, France and England, who seemed to have transferred their hereditary hatred from the Old World to the New, had been long struggling to obtain undivided dominion over the northern portion of the latter. Backed by Indian allies, who leagued themselves with one or the other, as they were influenced by caprice or a desire to prostrate some hostile tribe, these two great powers engaged in a desperate struggle for supremacy. The whole of Canada, Illinois, and the territory thence to the borders of the Mississippi were then claimed by the French, while the English occupied most of the countrv east of the Alleghany Mountains.

Both nations found efficient auxiliaries among the Indian tribes. On the side of the English were the Iroquois, called by them the Six Nations. These combined tribes formed the most powerful savage confederacy then existing on the Continent. It consisted of the Onondagas, the Cayugas, the Senecas, the Oneidas, and the Mohawks, and in 1712 the Tuscaroras of North Carolina were received into the league. Their domain embraced a very extensive tract of country, and from time to time it was enlarged by new conquests. They were robust and muscular, and delighted in ornamenting their persons with the finery so highly prized by the Indians, such as medals, ribands, the skins of wild beasts, and porcupine quills dyed of various colours. They possessed great energy, decision, and perseverance, and, when excited, were remarkable for the force and eloquence with which they spoke. Towards the west they claimed supremacy over the country as far as the Mississippi, and towards the northwest as far as Hudson's Bay; in short, all that was not occupied by the Southern Indians, the Sioux, the Knisteneaux, and the Chippewas.* Their affairs were conducted with more system than those of the more western tribes. Every year they held a grand council, consisting of representatives from each

* Schoolcraft's Discourse.

nation, at Onondaga, in the present state of New-York. Their youth were taught to bend the bow before their muscles were sufficiently strong to propel the arrow to its mark, and to grapple with the wild beasts of the forests as they would with the French, or their enemies the Algonquins. The cause of their attachment to the English is not known; but it was probably in part caprice, and partly a desire to overthrow the power of their rivals who have been mentioned. When their naked and painted warriors appeared on the edge of the forest, it was always a signal that mischief was at hand. "We are born free: we neither depend on Onondio nor Corlaer" (France nor England), said Haaskouan to De la Barre in 1684, and the course they pursued was the acting out of this declaration.

The Algonquins, on the other hand, were the allies of the French. The territory of this nation extended from Lake Erie along the whole chain of the upper lakes to Lake Winnipeg and Hudson's Bay on the north, and to the mouth of the Ohio River on the south. They were connected with the tribes immediately east of the St. Lawrence, and with those in the interior of New-England.* There were two powerful tribes, however, which were not connected with this league, the

* Schoolcraft's Discourse.

Hurons and the Foxes. The Hurons were of Iroquois origin, but, from causes which are not known they had severed from that confederacy, and taken part with the French; while the Foxes, who were of the Algonquin race, sided with the English. The causes of the friendship entertained by the Algonquins residing on the borders of the lakes for the former are obvious. The French mingled familiarly with them, and endeavoured by all possible means to secure their good-will. The traders visited their villages and took to themselves Indian wives. The Jesuit missionaries erected chapels in their camps, presented to them sculptured images, styling them their patron saints, held the crucifix before the dying, offered up their devotions with them before the picture of the Virgin, and planted the cross upon their graves. The French and Indians hunted together, lodged in the same wigwam, and drank from the same cup. On the contrary, the English were cold, distant, and forbidding in their manners: how, then, could the Algonquins be friendly to them, or how the enemies of the French?

For a long time these savages had been sent out into the neighbouring wilderness to attack the feeble settlements upon their borders, and to bring back the scalps of their murdered victims. Many a spot was wetted with the blood of its unfortunate inhabitants, and many a red column of British regulars wavered before the rifles of the combined French and Indians, covered by some swamp, or fighting from behind a breastwork of fallen trees The forests were often lighted up by the conflagration of burning villages, and the midnight solitude was startled by the shrieks of females under the tomahawk or scalping-knife, and mocked by human fiends, whose horrid thirst for blood was no less insatiable than that of the wolves which howled about their camps.

It was at length determined by the British government to make a powerful effort to possess themselves of the French colonies. Both France and England, it will be recollected, claimed these countries on the same grounds: that is, original discovery, conquest, and appropriation.

In 1757 the Earl of Chatham projected a campaign of a very formidable character against the French colonies, and the last great struggle soon commenced. Twelve thousand British soldiers arrived in this country under the command of General Amherst; and, at the same time, bodies of rangers, trained to the mode of fighting peculiar to the French and Indians, and also to the hardships of the forest, or what was called the "woods service," were brought into the field under the command of a citizen of New-Hampshire, Major

Robert Rogers, to co-operate with the British regulars and the colonial troops.*

Numerous positions having been occupied along the lake shores and the borders of the French colonies, in 1759 it was determined to bring the question to a speedy and decisive issue. It was proposed to divide the English army into three parts, and to penetrate to the very heart of Canada in three different directions, with a view to overthrow the French power at a single blow. Brigadier-general Wolfe, a young and gallant officer, was ordered to ascend the St. Lawrence and lay siege to Quebec. The duty assigned to General Amherst was to seize on Ticonderoga and Crown Point, and thence to proceed by the way of Lake Champlain and the St. Lawrence River to Quebec, to co-operate with General Wolfe in the siege of that place. The third division of the army, under the command of General Prideaux, was destined to attack Niagara, and, after obtaining possession of it, to be embarked on Lake Ontario, and proceed against Montreal. If that city should surrender before Quebec, General Prideaux was to unite his forces with those of General Wolfe, under the walls of the latter. General Amherst, after making great exertions, was obliged to retire into winter-quarters without accomplishing his object. Gen-

* Marshall.

eral Prideaux, as he had been directed, advanced against Niagara, which was garrisoned by a body of French troops from Detroit, Venango, and Presque Isle, and succeeded in capturing that post.*

The most difficult and important branch of the attack had been intrusted to Wolfe. The English fleet, having on board eight thousand men, under the command of this general, soon reached the Island of Orleans, opposite to Quebec, in the St. Lawrence River. The French force amounted to nine thousand men. The English were led on by a young officer, whose war-cry, like that of Nelson at a later period, was "Victory or Westminster Abbey." The first attack made by him was upon Montmorenci, where his troops were landed under cover of a fire from the ships-of-war. Here at last, then, on the broad St. Lawrence, were unfurled the hostile banners of these great rival nations. The glory of the two crowns was at stake. The cross of England glowed brightly upon its crimson ground, amid martial music, and floating above thousands of muskets glittering in the beams of the morning sun. Nor was the French force wanting in the gallantry which distinguished their opponents. The lilies embroidered upon the folds of their flag were borne aloft in triumph above

* Marshall.

hearts as brave as ever beat in human bosoms. Tribes of savages were seen armed and painted for the struggle which was to decide the destinies of these mighty rivals. The French force was commanded by a gallant and chivalrous officer, the Marquis de Montcalm. Before them lay the great river of Canada; beside them were the walls of Quebec, the stronghold of their power; and at a distance were seen the Falls of Montmorenci, glittering like a sheet of molten silver as they tumbled from the cliffs.

The effective force under Montcalm consisted of about ten thousand men, and his position was defended by floating batteries and armed vessels. Wolfe, by way of stratagem, sailed nine miles up the river, in order to distract the attention of the French army; when the French commander detached M. Bougainville with a strong force to that point, to prevent the English from landing. But about midnight the boats of the British ships floated silently down the St. Lawrence, and, being hailed by the French sentinels who were stationed on its banks with the cry of "Who comes there?" the English, who knew their watchword, replied "*La France*," and were suffered to proceed unmolested to their point of debarcation.*

At about four o'clock in the morning the British

* Smollet.

troops began to land, not having been discovered in their progress down the river. Soon after they commenced ascending the precipitous declivity which leads to the Heights of Abraham. They were protected by two fieldpieces, and their front was covered by the Royal Americans, a corps raised in New-York and New-England, as also by a reserve of one regiment, and the light infantry. They soon gained the heights and prepared for battle. The Marquis de Montcalm, the moment he discovered the English troops in possession of these important heights, sallied from Beauport with only a single fieldpiece. The two hostile armies soon met. The Canadian marksmen and Indian allies, no less expert with the rifle, were detached by the French commander to conceal themselves among the bushes and cornfields, from which they could most effectually annoy the enemy. The French troops advanced with great firmness, although composed for the most part of raw and undisciplined militia. As soon as they had reached within about two hundred yards of the British line, they commenced a sharp but irregular fire, supported by the Indians and the Canadian marksmen, who with their rifles did great execution. But they were met by that unshaken courage and obstinate determination which are characteristic of British soldiers; and the Scotch Highlanders, with their broadswords, making terrible havoc in their ranks, the French columns began to waver. General Wolfe, in the commencement of the action, received a bullet in his wrist while gallantly leading his men to the charge ; but, winding a handkerchief about the wound, he continued to fight on as though nothing had occurred. A second ball soon after struck him in the breast, and he fell. While leaning his head on the shoulder of one of his officers, he was startled from the lethargy of death by shouts from his ranks : "They fly! they fly!" "Who fly?" he faintly inquired. "The French," was the reply. "Then," said he, "I die happy;" and his spirit departed amid the thunders of the battle. The Marquis de Montcalm, the commander of the French army, was also mortally wounded, and died a few days after the engagement. Monuments have been erected to these two heroes in the city of Quebec. The remains of the French army, retiring to Montreal, demanded a capitulation, which was granted. Accordingly, in November, 1760, articles of agreement were entered into between General Amherst and the Marquis de Vaudreuil, by which the latter surrendered to the crown of England Detroit, Michilimackinac, and all the posts within the government of Canada that were in possession of the French.

A few days after the signing of this capitulation,

Major Rogers was detached by General Amherst, at the head of a competent force, to take possession of the distant posts on the frontier, to administer to the French inhabitants there the oath of allegiance, and effectually to establish the power of England in place of that of France. He was ordered to embark his troops in boats on Lake Erie, stopping on his way at Presque Isle, to make known to the officer of that post the instructions he had received. He was also the bearer of despatches to Brigadier-general Monkton, which he was to deliver, and receive from that officer his final orders as to the manner in which he should proceed to take possession of Detroit, Michilimackinac, and the other French posts. Having accomplished the objects of the expedition, he was to return in compliance with the orders that might be given him by General Monkton, transport his boats across the portage of Niagara Falls into Lake Ontario, where they were to be delivered into the hands of his commanding officer, and thence he was to march his detachment by land to Albany.*

In obedience to these instructions, Major Rogers embarked the force assigned him in fifteen whale-boats at Montreal. On arriving at Fort Frontenac he met with a party of Indians who were out upon a hunting excursion, and communicated to

* Rogers's Journal.

them the first news of the capitulation. They found these savages friendly, and were supplied by them with wild-fowl and venison. Soon after they fell in with another body of about fifty Indians, on a stream which flows into Lake Ontario, where they were taking salmon. They all appeared to be gratified with the intelligence that the French had surrendered the country. After arriving at Toronto, the detachment were not long in reaching Niagara, where they provided themselves with moccasins, blankets, and such other articles as were necessary for the expedition. Proceeding on their way to Detroit, they soon reached Presque Isle, from which point Rogers embarked in a canoe, and proceeded to the old site of Fort Duquesne, now called Pittsburgh. Here he found Brigadier-general Monkton, and delivered to him the despatches he had brought from General Amherst. A detachment of Royal Americans, or colonial troops, under Capt. Campbell, were marched from this post for the purpose of aiding him in so hazardous an expedition. At the same time, an officer was ordered to drive forty fat cattle from Presque Isle to Detroit, where it was supposed they would be wanted by the troops. Captain Wait was also sent back to Niagara for provisions, and directed on his return to coast along the northern shore of Lake Erie, and encamp about twenty miles east of Detroit. Thus started the first English military expedition that had ever ventured upon the western shore of Lake Erie, for the purpose of wresting from the French their possessions in these distant regions.*

At this time appeared Pontiac, a chief who was destined to figure largely in the history of this territory at a subsequent period. His residence was Pechee Island, which looks out upon the waters of Lake St. Clair, about eight miles above the city of Detroit. An Ottawa by birth, and belonging to a tribe which claimed to be the oldest in this quarter, he was greatly esteemed both by the English and French. Thus his influence was greater than that of any other individual among the lake tribes. His personal qualities, indeed, were such as to ensure respect; and he possessed, moreover, hereditary claims to authority, according to the customs of the Indians. His form was cast in the finest mould of savage grace and strength, and his eye seemed capable of penetrating at a glance the secret motives which actuated the tribes around him. Such was Pontiac, the daring chief who was about to dispute the English claims to the territory of the lakes. He could not endure the sight of this people driving the game from his hunting-grounds, and his old friends and

* Rogers's Journal.

allies, the French, from the lands they had so long possessed. Accordingly, when he was apprized that an English detachment was advancing along the lakes to take possession of the country, he could not restrain his indignation. Forthwith he despatched a body of Ottawas from Detroit, with a message to the English, who were then encamped at the mouth of Chocage River, informing them that Pontiac, the king of the country where they were, was approaching, and requesting them to stop until he should arrive. Pontiac, on reaching the English camp, demanded of Rogers the business on which he had come, and how he dared to enter his country without his permission. Major Rogers replied that he had no design against the Indians, and that his only object was the removal of the French, who had hitherto been the means of preventing all friendly relations between his tribes and the English. Pontiac then gave him to understand that he should stand in his path until the morning, and at the same time presented him with a small string of wampum, signifying that he forbade the English detachment from advancing any farther without his permission. He also told Major Rogers that if he was in want of any food, he would send his warriors, and they should procure it for him.*

* Rogers's Journal.

A council having in the mean time been held, Pontiac made his appearance in the English camp the next morning, saying that he had the most friendly disposition towards the English, and he smoked the pipe of peace with their commander. At the same time, he informed Rogers that he would protect him against a party of Indians who had stationed themselves at the mouth of the Detroit River, and he sent also several of his warriors to assist Captain Brewer in bringing on the cattle which he was driving to Detroit. In addition to this, he despatched messengers to the Indians encamped on the Detroit River, and to those on the north and west shores of Lake Erie, to inform them that he had given the English permission to pass through his territory; and, still farther to evince his friendship, he supplied them with venison, wild turkeys, and several bags of parched corn.*

Encamping at some distance from the mouth of the Detroit River, Rogers despatched the following letter to M. Bellestre, the French commandant at Detroit:

"*To Captain Bellestre, or the Officer commanding at Detroit.*

"Sir:—That you may not be alarmed at the ap-

* Rogers's Journal.

proach of the English troops under my command when I come to Detroit, I send forward this by Lieut. Brheme, to acquaint you that I have General Amherst's orders to take possession of Detroit and such other posts as are in that district, which, by capitulation agreed to and signed by Marquis de Vaudreuil and General Amherst, the 8th of September last, now belong to Great Britain. I have with me the Marquis de Vaudreuil's letters to you, directed for your guidance on this occasion, which letters I shall deliver you when I am at or near your post, and shall encamp the troops I have with me at some distance from the fort, till you have reasonable time to be made acquainted with the Marquis de Vaudreuil's instructions and the capitulation, a copy of which I have with me likewise.

"I am, sir, your humble servant,

"ROBERT ROGERS."

After this he encamped with his detachment on a stream which empties into Lake Erie. Here he found a number of Huron chiefs, who inquired of him whether the reports which they had heard in regard to the surrender of the territory were true; apprizing him, at the same time, that they had been sent out by M. Bellestre for the purpose of defending the country, and to obtain information as to the events which had transpired below.

Rogers confirmed the fact of the capitulation, and made a speech to the Hurons of the most conciliatory character; after which he encamped at the west end of Lake Erie with his detachment. The next day he met with a party of Indians, who told him that Bellestre was "a strong man," and that he intended to fight the English. Not long after, sixty Indians, who said that they had come from Detroit the previous day, arrived at his camp. They offered to conduct the English detachment to that place, and informed Rogers that M. Brheme, who had been sent by him with the letter, had been imprisoned by the French commandant.*

While the English were thus advancing towards Detroit, the French commandant was not idle. He had collected round his post numerous tribes of savages, and, knowing that they were strongly impressed by symbols, he had caused a pole to be erected, with the image of a man's head on the top, and upon this was placed a crow. He told the Indians that the head represented the English, and the crow himself, and that the meaning of it all was, that the French would scratch out the brains of their enemies. The Indians, however, would not believe it, and expressed their apprehensions that the reverse would be the fact, and that the English at Detroit would scratch out the brains of the French.

* Rogers's Journal.

About this time Rogers received the following letter from the commandant of Detroit:

"SIR:—I received the letter you wrote me by one of your officers, but, as I have no interpreter, cannot fully answer it. The officer that delivered me yours gives me to understand that he was sent to give me notice of your arrival to take possession of this garrison, according to the capitulation made in Canada; that you have likewise a letter from Monsieur Vaudreuil directed to me. I beg, sir, you will halt your troops at the entrance of the river till you send me the capitulation and the Marquis de Vaudreuil's letter, that I may act in conformity thereto.

"I have the honour to be, &c., &c.,

"DE BELLESTRE."

Shortly after, on the 25th of November, the English commander received the letter inserted below from M. Bellestre:

"DETROIT, 25th Nov., 1760.

"SIR: — I have already, by Mr. Barrager, acquainted you with the reasons why I could not answer particularly the letter which was delivered me the 22d instant by the officer you sent to me. I am entirely unacquainted with the reasons of his not returning to you. I sent my Huron interpreter to that nation, and told him to stop them should they be on the road, not knowing positively whether they were inclined to favour you or us; and to tell them from me they should behave peaceably; that I knew what I owed to my general, and that, when the capitulation should be settled, I was obliged to obey. The said interpreter has orders to wait on you and deliver you this.

"Be not surprised, sir, if along the coast you find the inhabitants upon their guard. It was told them you had several Indian nations with you, to whom you had promised permission to plunder; nay, that they were even resolved to force you to it. I have therefore allowed the said inhabitants to take to their arms, as it is for your safety and preservation as well as ours; for, should those Indians become insolent, you may not, perhaps, in your present situation, be able to subdue them alone.

"I flatter myself, sir, that, as soon as this shall come to hand, you will send me, by some of the gentlemen you have with you, both the capitulation and Monsieur de Vaudreuil's letter

"I have the honour to be, sir,

"Your very humble and obedient servant,

"De Bellestre."

After advancing five miles farther up the Detroit River, Rogers the next day sent a second letter, of which the following is a copy, by Captain Campbell:

"SIR:—I acknowledge the receipt of your two letters, both of which were delivered to me yesterday. Mr. Brheme has not yet returned. The enclosed letter from the Marquis de Vaudreuil will inform you of the surrender of all Canada to the King of Great Britain, and of the great indulgence granted to the inhabitants, as also of the terms granted to the troops of his most Christian majesty. Capt. Campbell, whom I have sent forward with this letter, will show you the capitulation. I desire you will not detain him, as I am determined, agreeable to my instructions from General Amherst, speedily to relieve your post. I shall stop the troops I have with me at the hither end of the town till four o'clock, by which time I expect your answer. Your inhabitants will not surprise me: as yet, I have seen no other in that position but savages waiting for my orders. I can assure you, sir, the inhabitants of Detroit shall not be molested, they and you complying with the capitulation, but be protected in the quiet and peaceable enjoyment of their estates; neither shall they be pillaged by my Indians, nor by yours that have joined me.

"I am, &c., ROBERT ROGERS

"To Captain Bellestre,
Commanding at Detroit."

After despatching this letter he pushed his boats up the Detroit River to within half a mile of the fort, and encamped his detachment in a field.

The English camp was soon visited by Captain Campbell and a French officer, who presented to Major Rogers M. Bellestre's compliments, stating that he was instructed by that officer to inform him that the post had been surrendered. Lieutenant Lefflie and M'Cormick were then sent with thirty-six Royal Americans, who immediately took possession of the fort; when the Indians, to the number of seven hundred, who had been collected there by the French commander, set up a tremendous yell, exulting that their prophecy concerning the crow had been verified.

Major Rogers now formally took possession of this important post, receiving at the same time a plan of the fort, and a list of the warlike and other stores. The French commandant and the troops forming the garrison were placed under the charge of Lieutenant Holmes, with thirty Rangers, to be conducted to Philadelphia. Twenty men were also sent to escort the French soldiers from the posts of Miami and Gatanois, and the command of the fort was given to Captain Campbell. Rogers, having made a treaty with the neighbouring Indians, set out with a party to Lake Huron for the purpose of taking possession of Michilimackinac;

but the ice in the lake so obstructed his passage that he could not proceed by water, and the Indians told him that it would be impossible for him to reach that place by land without snow-shoes. Accordingly, having replaced the ammunition and stores which he had taken with him at Detroit, he left that post on the 21st of November, 1760, after intrusting to Captain Campbell its command. With the change of jurisdiction thus effected, a new scene will now open upon us.*

* Rogers's Journal.

CHAPTER V.

Condition of the Territory under the English.—Pontiac forms a Confederacy to attack the English Posts.—War breaks out.—Siege of Detroit.—Battle of Bloody Bridge.—Indians assemble around Michilimackinac.—Minavavana—Alexander Henry—Wawatam.—Michilimackinac destroyed.—General Bradstreet arrives.—Peace concluded.—Death of Pontiac.

No material change took place in the condition of the country in consequence of its surrender to the English. The capitulation of Montreal permitted the French emigrants to remain in the territory, and to enjoy undisturbed their civil and religious rights. Agriculture was no more encouraged than before, and the same general plan continued to be pursued in conducting the fur-trade. No land was allowed to be purchased directly of the Indians, nor were the English commandants, styled governors, permitted to make any grants of land except within certain prescribed limits. The settlements of the French, however, continued to extend, and their long, narrow farms, surrounded by pickets, and fronted by houses of bark or logs, and their roofs thatched with straw, were seen stretching along the banks of all the principal streams. There were as yet no schools, and the instruction of the children continued to be confided entirely to the Catholic priests.* Before that time peltries had constituted almost the only medium of traffic, but now English coin began to be introduced. Horses were for a long time unknown at Detroit, the first having been brought there, it is said, from Fort Duquesne, after Braddock's defeat.†

Although the English had acquired possession of the country, it had been against the will of the Indians. The design of Pontiac probably was to lead the English into his territory only that he might have a better opportunity to destroy them. He believed that it was their intention to drive him from his lands, and he therefore considered them as dangerous intruders. His spacious domain, its waters abounding with fish and its woods with game, had now fallen into the hands of a people whom he had always looked upon as his enemy. Some of the Indians had been struck by the British officers in the garrison, an indignity which their savage natures could not endure, and they readily joined with their chief to expel these hated strangers from their country.

Pontiac was not long in circulating war-belts among all the principal tribes on the borders of the lakes, and he formed a chain of operations extend-

* Manuscript Journals from Detroit.

† See Manuscript Journals.

ing more than a thousand miles along their waters. He flattered himself that, if the British garrisons could be destroyed or driven away, he should afterward be able effectually to defend the country against farther intrusion by means of his own strength, combined with that of his savage allies. A grand council of the Indians was accordingly soon assembled at the River Aux Ecorce, and Pontiac addressed them in person. He told them that it was the design of the English to drive the Indians from their country, and that they were their natural and inveterate enemies. He also assured them that the Great Spirit had appeared to a Delaware Indian in a dream, and thus addressed him: "Why do you suffer these dogs in red clothing" (the English) "to enter your country and take the land I gave you? Drive them from it; and then, when you are in distress, I will help you." He also exhibited to them a war-belt, which he said the French king had sent over from France, ordering them to drive out the British, and make way for the return of the French.*

The shores of the lakes were soon alive with bodies of Indian warriors, who had abandoned their hunting-grounds and camps, and were repairing to the posts on the frontier. Among these were seen the Ottawas, the Chippewas, the Miamis, the Pot-

* Cass.

tawatamies, the Missisagas, the Shawanese, the Ottagamies, and the Winnebagoes, besides parties from numerous other tribes. At about the same time they attacked the Forts of Le Bœuf, Venango, Presque Isle, Michilimackinac, St. Joseph, Miami, Green Bay, Ouiatonon, Pittsburgh, and Sandusky. Their military operations, indeed, extended along the entire line of the waters of the lower lakes.*

This general and simultaneous attack was made in the month of May, 1763, and was so sudden and wholly unexpected that the garrisons were all taken by surprise. Detroit was then the most important station upon the lakes, and was garrisoned by one hundred and twenty-two men and eight officers, Major Gladwin being the commandant. Three rows of pickets surrounded the fort in the form of a square. Most of the houses of the French were situated within these pickets, that they might be protected by the guns of the fort. The inhabitants were provided with arms and ammunition Within the pickets there was also a circular space, which was named by the French *Le chemin du Ronde*, from its being a place of deposite for arms; and over the gates of the fort, and at each of its corners, there were small dwellings. The town was defended in front by an armed schooner named

* See Cass.

the Beaver, moored in the river, which at this point is about three quarters of a mile wide. The post commanded the great channel of communication from Lake Michigan to Buffalo and Pittsburgh; its possession, therefore, was an object of great importance; and Pontiac, who was the chief director of the confederacy, undertook its reduction in person.*

His plan was one which strikingly exhibits the cunning which is so characteristic of the Indians. He intended to take the fort by surprise; and for this purpose he ordered a party of his warriors to saw off their rifles so short that they could conceal them under their blankets, and under a feigned pretence to gain admission into the fort, and massacre the garrison. To carry out his design, he encamped at a short distance from the post, and sent word to the commandant that he was desirous of holding a council with him, that "they might brighten the chain of peace." On the evening of that day, an Indian woman, by the name of Catharine, brought to Major Gladwin a pair of moccasins which she had been employed to make for him, and he was so much pleased with them that he gave her an elk-skin, and told her to take it home and make from it several pairs more. She took the skin, but continued to linger about the gate

* Cass.

of the fort as if her business were unfinished; and the singularity of her conduct attracted attention. Major Gladwin accordingly ordered her to be called back, and inquired of her why she did not hasten home, that she might finish the moccasins by the time he had required them to be done. The woman remarked that she did not like to take the skin away, as he seemed to prize it so much, since she feared "*she could never bring it back.*" Her mind seemed to be struggling with some secret, and, after being pressed, she developed the whole plot. Major Gladwin immediately ordered the guards to be doubled, and sentinels to be stationed on the ramparts.

As night approached, fires were seen in the Indian camp, and their war-songs were distinctly heard, so that the English commandant was convinced that something important was contemplated by them, and that the woman had told the truth, as the savages always excite themselves in this manner preparatory to any great enterprise they are about to undertake.

The next morning, according to previous arrangement, Pontiac and his warriors repaired to the fort. As he was advancing, he noticed that there was an unusual number of soldiers upon the ramparts, and that the officers all had pistols in their belts. Having entered the council-house, or the place assigned for the meeting, he opened the discussion with a speech, in which he made great professions of friendship for the English. As the time approached when, as the woman had stated, the belt was to be delivered, and a fire upon the garrison commenced, his gestures became more vehement. At this moment the governor and his officers drew their swords, and the English soldiers made a clattering upon the ground with their muskets: Pontiac himself was now the party surprised, but he continued perfectly calm and unmoved.

The commandant soon commenced his reply, but, instead of thanking the chief for his professions of friendship, he charged him with being a traitor, and, to convince him of his knowledge of the plot, he stepped forward to the Indian who sat on his skin nearest to him, and, opening his blanket, exposed the shortened rifle. At the same time, addressing himself to the warriors, he told them instantly to leave the fort, as his men, should they discover their treachery, would show them no mercy. He also assured them that they would be permitted to go out in safety, as he had promised them his protection.*

The warriors accordingly sallied out of the fort; but, as soon as they had passed the gates, they

* Cass.

turned about and fired upon the garrison. They then proceeded to the commons, where they murdered an English woman who resided there, and, horrid to relate, cooked and feasted upon her remains. After this they went to Isle de Cochon (Hog Island), and barbarously destroyed a whole family.

The savages had now sufficiently evinced their hostile intentions. Collecting around the fort, they fired upon the garrison from the nearest houses, and even from behind the pickets. Measures were soon taken, however, to burn such buildings as they could avail themselves of for this purpose, by throwing shells. But, as soon as the shells fell, the savages ran up to them, with loud yells, and extinguished the matches before they had time to explode. Still, in spite of all their efforts to prevent it, the buildings were soon demolished, and the Indians then withdrew to a low ridge which overlooked the pickets, and from this they kept up a constant fire upon the fort.*

Although Pontiac, as the acknowledged head of the confederacy, was the leader in the attack upon Detroit, he was aided by several chiefs, who had placed themselves under his direction. Among these were the Ottawa chiefs *Mahigam,* or the Wolf, *Wabunemay,* or the White Sturgeon, *Kitta-*

* Cass.

comsi, and *Agouchiois;* and the Chippewa chiefs *Pashquois*, *Gayashque*, *Wasson*, and *Macatay-wasson*.

The influence of Pontiac had for a long time been very great, not only with the French, but also with the remotest tribes upon the borders of the lakes. In 1746 he defended Detroit against a combined force under Mackinac, the Turtle, aided by a portion of his own tribe, the Ottawas. While he was thus assisting the French, they were no less warm in their attachment to their allies. "When the French arrived at these falls" (the Sault de Ste. Marie), said a Chippewa chief, "they came and kissed us. They called us children, and we found them fathers. We lived like brethren in the same lodge. They never mocked our ceremonies; they never molested the places of our dead. Seven generations have passed away, but we have not forgotten it. Just, very just, were they towards us."

The siege of Detroit by Pontiac continued. Sometimes blazing arrows were launched from the bows of his warriors upon the Chapel for the purpose of burning it; and this they would have effected had they not been deterred from farther attempts by a Jesuit, who persuaded them that such an act would call down the vengeance of the Great Spirit. A breach was now attempted to be made in the pickets, and in this Major Gladwin co-operated with them, by ordering his men to cut them away from the inside, so that it was soon accomplished; but no sooner was it filled with the Indians than a small brass cannon, which had been brought to bear upon this point, was discharged upon them, and made terrible havoc. After this the fort was simply blockaded and its supplies cut off, by which means great suffering was occasioned to the garrison. Among the killed on the side of the English was Sir Robert Devers, whose body was boiled and eaten by the savages. Captain Robertson experienced a similar fate, and of the skin of one of his arms a tobacco-pouch was made.

Major Campbell, it will be recollected, had been appointed to the command of the fort by Major Rogers, and it was a great point with the savages to get possession of the person of this officer, as he was much esteemed, not only by the French and English, but by the Indians also, for his chivalrous character, and, therefore, the more valuable as a hostage. Pontiac accordingly solicited an interview with this officer, that, as he stated, "they might smoke the pipe of peace together." Two French citizens recommended this interview, and were, in fact, made the agents of Pontiac to effect it. The Indian chief, in the mean time, solemnly promised that the English commandant should be permitted to return in safety to the fort. The proposal was acceded to; but no sooner had Pontiac got his enemy into his hands, than his promise was entirely forgotten, and he told him that his life even should not be spared but on the condition that the fort was surrendered. The conduct of Pontiac in this transaction had been such as to destroy all confidence in his word. The fate of this brave and generous officer was truly melancholy. An Ottawa chief had been killed in the siege of Michilimackinac, and his nephew hastened to Detroit to seek for revenge. Here meeting with Major Campbell, he instantly killed him with a blow of his tomahawk. The murderer fled to Saginaw to escape the vengeance of Pontiac.*

The Beaver, the armed vessel to which allusion has been made, had been sent to Niagara for the purpose of hastening the arrival of a re-enforcement of men, and to procure a supply of provisions. Lieutenant Cuyler, with ninety-seven men, was sent from that post with supplies, and, apprehending no danger, they had landed at Point Pelée and encamped. Here they were discovered by the Indians, and at dawn the next morning they were attacked, and the whole party either cut off or taken prisoners, with the exception of one officer and thirty men, who succeeded in gaining a barge, in which they crossed Lake Erie and reached San-

* Cass.

dusky Bay. The savages placed their prisoners on board the boats, and compelled them to manage them, escorting them in triumph to Detroit, along the Canadian bank of the river. When they were near this place, four British soldiers determined to make their escape, and for this purpose changed the course of the boat they were in, setting up at the same time a loud cry. After some resistance their Indian guards leaped overboard, one of them dragging a soldier along with him, and they both were drowned. The remaining three were now fired on by the Indians in the other boats, and also by those on the bank of the river, though without any other effect than wounding one of their number. In the mean time, the armed schooner on the Detroit side opened a fire upon the savages, which dispersed their boats, and likewise the guard upon the opposite shore. The rest of the prisoners were taken by the Indians to Hog Island, and there put to death.*

The French residents themselves did not escape wholly unharmed amid these scenes of savage violence. Maintaining a neutral position in the war, they were regarded with no little jealousy by their former allies of the Algonquin race. Their houses were in several instances broken open, and their cattle plundered by Pontiac's warriors, though the

* Cass.

Ottawa chief gave to the sufferers certificates of indemnity for all such losses, formed of pieces of bark, on which was drawn the figure of an otter, the emblem of his tribe, and these pledges were all faithfully redeemed at a subsequent period.*

The savages, finding that all their attempts to destroy the fort were unavailing, endeavoured to engage the French in the alliance; and for this purpose Pontiac assembled a council of his warriors and of the French inhabitants at the River Aux Ecorce, on which occasion he addressed to them the following speech:

"My Brothers:—I have no doubt that this war is very troublesome to you, and that my warriors, who are continually passing and repassing through your settlements, frequently kill your cattle and injure your property. I am sorry for it, and hope you do not think I am pleased with this conduct of my young men; and, as a proof of my friendship, remember the war you had seventeen years ago (1746), and the part I took in it. The Northern nations combined together and came to destroy you. Who defended you? Was it not myself and my young men? The great chief Machinac (the Turtle) said in council that he would carry to his native village the head of your chief warrior, and that he would eat his heart and drink

* Drake.

his blood. Did I not then join you, and go to his camp and say to him, that if he wished to kill the French, he must pass over my body and the bodies of my young men? Did I not take up the tomahawk with you? aid you in fighting your battles with Mackinac, and in driving him home to his country? Why do you think I would turn my arms against you? Am I not the same French Pontiac who assisted you seventeen years ago? I am a Frenchman, and I wish to die a Frenchman.

"My brothers," continued Pontiac, throwing a war-belt into the midst of the council, "I begin to grow tired of this bad meat which is upon our lands, but I see that this is not your case; for, instead of assisting us in our war with the English, you are actually assisting them. I have already told you, and I now tell you again, that when I undertook this war, it was only your interest I sought, and that I knew what I was about. I yet know what I am about. This year they must all perish: the Master of Life so orders it. His will is known to us, and we must do as he says. And you, my brothers, who know him better than we do, wish to oppose his will. Until now I have avoided urging you upon this subject, in the hope that, if you could not aid, you would not injure us. I did not wish to ask you to fight with us against the English, and I did not believe that you would take part with them. You will say you are not with them. I know it; but your conduct amounts to the same thing. You tell them all we do, and you carry our counsels and plans to them. Now take your choice. You must be entirely French, like ourselves, or entirely English. If you are French, take this belt for yourselves and for your young men, and join us. If you are English, we declare war against you."

Previous to this, and on the third of June, 1763, news had been received of the conclusion of peace between France and England; and one of the French inhabitants, holding up a copy of the treaty in answer to this harangue, replied, "My brother, you see that our arms are tied by our great father, the King of France: untie this knot, and we will join you; but, till that is done, we shall sit quietly on our mats."

The vessel which had been despatched to Niagara now returned with a supply of provisions and arms. To prevent her reaching the fort, a great number of Indians had left the siege and repaired to Fighting Island, a short distance below. After annoying her from their canoes at the mouth of the river, they at length resolved to get possession of her by boarding, and were approaching her with all their force for that purpose, when she opened upon them a destructive fire, which wounded and killed a large number, and put the rest to flight. She then dropped down the river to wait for a fair wind, and a few days afterward reached Detroit without farther molestation.*

Pontiac now endeavoured to destroy the vessels which were anchored opposite to the fort, as they greatly aided in its defence. He for this purpose demolished the barns of several of the French settlers, and from the materials, which were of a resinous nature and perfectly dry, he constructed rafts, and, setting them on fire, committed them to the current of the river, which is here quite rapid, in the expectation that they would float down against them and burn them. The English, however, perceiving his object, anchored small boats above the vessels, fastened to each other with iron chains, to intercept and turn away these dangerous masses, in which they were perfectly successful, and the blazing rafts passed harmlessly by.

It was not long, however, before efficient aid was received by the English garrison. A fleet of gun-boats made its appearance, strongly armed, and having on board a detachment of three hundred regular troops, under the command of Captain Dalyell, one of the aids of Sir Jeffry Amherst. Supposing that Pontiac might be surprised

* Cass.

in his camp, they landed a force of two hundred and forty-seven men, and marched up the river with that object. But this chief, apprized of their intentions, had removed his women and children, and prepared for a vigorous defence. A party of his warriors were concealed behind the pickets of the neighbouring farms, others lay hid in the long prairie grass, which grew here to a great height, and others, again, were concealed behind heaps of wood. The British force had no sooner reached the point now called Bloody Bridge, than they received a destructive fire from the rifles of the savages. For a moment their columns wavered, as their commander, Captain Dalyell, had fallen at the first discharge; but, soon rallying, they fought with great bravery, and charged upon the enemy with the bayonet. The Indians, however, without being seen, continued to pour forth a destructive fire upon the English, and could only be dislodged from their places of concealment by driving them from house to house and from field to field. Perceiving that their numbers were diminishing, and that they were fighting under great disadvantages, the English now commenced a retreat to the fort, protected by the armed gunboats, after a loss of nineteen men killed and forty-two wounded.*

While these scenes were passing at Detroit,

* Drake.

events of a still more tragical character were taking place on the upper lakes. Michilimackinac, which is distant nearly four hundred miles from Detroit, has been already described. This fort was surrounded with pickets of cedar, and its stockade was washed by the waves of the strait. At that time the fort was protected by several pieces of brass cannon, taken from the trading-posts of Hudson's Bay. There was a chapel in which mass was regularly performed by a Jesuit missionary. At this post there were about thirty families, and it was garrisoned by ninety-three men. The savages here were still more inveterate in their hostility to the English than at Detroit. Alexander Henry, the English trader, had been obliged to wear the garb of a coureur des bois on his way to that post, where there were then but four English merchants residing. The hostile disposition of the savages was, indeed, clearly manifested on his first arrival. He had been there but a very short time when he was visited by a body of Chippewas, painted and dressed in the most warlike style, with feathers thrust through their noses. Their chief, Minavavana, thus addressed him :*

"Englishman, it is to you that I speak, and I demand your attention.

* Henry.

"Englishman, you know that the French king is our father; he promised to be such, and we, in return, promised to be his children: this promise we have kept.

"Englishman, it is you that have made war with this our father. You are his enemy, and how, then, could you have the boldness to venture among us his children? You know that his enemies are ours.

"Englishman, we are informed that our father, the King of France, is old and infirm, and that, being fatigued with making war upon your nation, he has fallen asleep. During this sleep you have taken advantage of him, and possessed yourselves of Canada. But his nap is almost at an end: I think I hear him already stirring, and inquiring for his children the Indians; and when he does awake, what must become of you? He will destroy you utterly.

"Englishman, although you have conquered the French, you have not yet conquered us. We are not your slaves. These lakes, these woods and mountains, are left to us by our ancestors; they are our inheritance, and we will part with them to none. Your nation supposes that we, like the white people, cannot live without bread, and pork, and beef, but you ought to know that He, the Great Spirit and Master of Life, has provided food for us in these spacious lakes and on these wooded mountains.

"Englishman, our father, the King of France, employed our young men to make war upon your nation. In this war many of them have been killed, and it is our custom to retaliate until such time as the spirits of the slain are satisfied. But the spirits of the slain are only to be satisfied in one of two ways: the first is by spilling the blood of the nation by which they fell; the other, by covering the bodies of the dead, and thus allaying the resentment of their relations. This is done by making presents.

"Englishman, your king has never sent us any presents, nor entered into any treaty with us, wherefore he and we are still at war; and, while he does these things, we must consider that we have no other father or friend among the white people than the King of France. But for you, we have taken into consideration that you have ventured among us in the expectation that we should not molest you. You do not come armed with an intention to make war. You come in peace to trade with us, and supply us with necessaries of which we are much in want. We shall regard you, therefore, as a brother, and you may sleep tranquilly, without fear of the Chippewas. As a token of our friendship, we present you this pipe to smoke."

But, although no attack was made upon him, it

was perceived that the spirit of the savages was anything but friendly. He was afterward visited by a chief who was at the head of a party of Ottawa warriors, who also made him a speech, and compelled him to deliver a part of his goods to the Indians on a credit.

Thus affairs were here speedily coming to a crisis. The warriors in the wilderness around this post had also received from Pontiac the war-belt, and were now busy in collecting their bands for the purpose of joining his confederacy, the object of which was to blot out the English power from the territory bordering on the lakes. No serious suspicions were awakened at Michilimackinac, although large bodies of Indians had been noticed collecting around the post, some of them apparently for the purpose of purchasing European merchandise, trinkets, and silver ornaments which Henry had for sale, but for the most part without any apparent object.

On the seventh of June, Wawatam, a Chippewa chief, called on this trader, who had recently come from the Sault de Ste. Marie, telling him that he was sorry that he had left the Sault, and requesting that he would go back with him to that post the following day. He also desired to know if Major Etherington had not received some bad news; for, said he, "I have been disturbed with the noise of evil birds."* The following day he repeated his request, and urged his suspicions anew. The trader conceived it to be his duty to inform Major Etherington of what had taken place; but, unfortunately, this officer paid no attention to it, considering it as mere idle apprehension.

The number of the savages having greatly increased, it was proposed the next day to celebrate the anniversary of the king's birth by a game which is called *Baggatiway*. This is a common game among the Indians, and is played with bats and ball. A ball is placed in the centre of an open piece of ground; the players divide themselves into two parties, and a struggle then takes place between them to knock the ball to the post of the opposite party. It had been agreed among the savages to throw the ball, as if by accident, over the pickets; and, when this had been done, to rush after it, possess themselves of the fort, and massacre the garrison.*

The game was accordingly commenced, and Major Etherington, who was present as a spectator, laid a wager on the success of the Chippewas, the greater part of the garrison being at the same time collected outside the fort to witness the sport. Suddenly the ball, according to their previous understanding, was thrown over the pickets, and, as

* Henry.

appeared very natural, the Indians all rushed after it. But almost instantly the war-cry of the savages rose from the interior of the fort, and a dreadful scene commenced. The trader, who had been prevented from being present at the game, hearing the tumult without, and finding the savages, about four hundred in number, in possession of the post, crawled over a low fence which separated his house from that of M. Langlade, a French Canadian, and entreated him to afford him some place of concealment. But Langlade, shrugging up his shoulders, hastily turned away from the window where he had been looking out, coolly saying that he knew of no such place. At this moment a Pawnee slave belonging to Langlade beckoned to Henry to come to a door which she pointed out to him, conducted him to the garret of the house, and, having concealed him there, locked the door and took away the key.

Henry gazed through the crevices of the wall upon the scene below, and it was a scene of horror. A great number of the English soldiers lay dead around the fort; some were seen struggling between the knees of the savages, who were scalping them while yet alive. Others were cut in pieces, and their blood was drank by the warriors from the hollows of their hands joined together, while they were shrieking most hideously, like so many demons. At length there was a profound silence, an awful stillness, which denoted that, for want of more victims, the work of death was done.*

The Indians now gathered about the house of Langlade, and asked him if any of the English had taken shelter there. Langlade replied that none had to his knowledge, but that they might examine for themselves. Two or three of the savages coming to the garret door, demanded the key, and, unlocking it, went in

By this time Henry had concealed himself behind a heap of birch-bark vessels which were used in the making of maple-sugar, where the dark colour of his clothes, aided by the absence of light in the room, prevented him from being seen, so that the Indians, satisfying themselves that there was no one there, soon went away. There was a mat in the room, and Henry, laying himself down on it, soon fell asleep. It was not long, however, before he was awakened by the wife of Langlade, who informed him that most of the English had been despatched, but that he might hope to escape. The shades of night now came on, and the trader sought again in slumber to forget the horrors of the scene.

He was not, however, so easily to escape. Langlade's wife, notwithstanding the encouragement she

* Henry.

had held out to him, determined to make known his place of concealment, saying that the Indians would murder her if the trader was found secreted in her house. Accordingly, she took the key and gave it to Wenniway, a chief of the most hideous appearance. This warrior was more than six feet in height, and his naked body was painted all over with a mixture of grease and charcoal, as was his face, with the exception of a circular ring around each of his eyes.* Accompanied by a body of savages, he entered the garret, and approaching the trembling trader, grasped him by the collar, and fixing his eyes steadfastly upon him, raised his knife as if about to plunge it into his breast; but, suddenly checking himself, he dropped the fatal weapon and said, "I won't kill you. I have lost a brother whose name is Musinigon. You shall be called after him."

But the sufferings of the trader were not yet at an end. He was stripped of his clothes and carried to L'Arbre a Croche as a prisoner. Here, however, his friend Wawatam, faithful to his promise of protection, appeared in his behalf, ransomed him, and accompanied the trader to the island of Mackinaw, where he concealed him from a band of drunken savages in what is now called the Scull Rock.

* Henry.

The fort of Michilimackinac was now burned to the ground. Seventy of the English soldiers had been massacred, and, to complete the sanguinary deed, the bodies of many of them were boiled and eaten by the savages: the lives of the remainder, as well as of the prisoners taken at St. Joseph and Green Bay, were spared, and on the return of peace they were all released, either with or without ransom. At the close of these tragical events, a number of Indian canoes arrived with English traders, who were beaten, insulted, and marched to the prison lodge.

After the work of devastation had been finished, many of the Indians retired to the island of Mackinaw, while others repaired to Detroit, to aid Pontiac in the siege of this post. This chief, however, soon found that his enemies were too formidable for him. General Bradstreet now arrived to relieve the fort, at the head of an army of three thousand men. On his way he had destroyed the villages of the hostile savages, laid waste their cornfields along the rich bottoms of the Maumee, dispersed the natives in every direction, and reached Detroit without opposition. The Indians, perceiving that they could no longer contend against so powerful a foe, laid down their arms, and thus the war was brought to a close.

Of Pontiac after his discomfiture, but little is

certainly known. Disappointed and mortified at the failure of his plans, he retired to Illinois, where he was assassinated about the year 1767 by an Indian of the Peoria tribe.* The character of this chief was bold and strongly marked. Excelled by none of his race in courage, strength, and energy, he possessed traits which pointed him out for a leader. To have had sufficient influence to bring the numerous tribes of the West, along a frontier of a thousand miles, to co-operate with him in his desperate undertaking, must have required much more than ordinary talents. Although destitute of those principles of honour which prevail among civilized nations in the operations of war, he possessed a larger share of humanity than is commonly found among savages. Undismayed by difficulties, and far-seeing and comprehensive in his plans, he fought from a sense of justice and in defence of the rich domain which had been bequeathed to him by his ancestors.

* Cass.

CHAPTER VI.

Condition of the Fur-trade under the English.—Hudson's Bay Company.—English Administration of the Law.—Criminal Trial.—Quebec Act.—Mineral Rock on Lake Superior.—Northwest Company.—American Revolution.—Expeditions from Detroit.—Indian Council held at Detroit.—American Independence established.

FROM the year 1679, when La Salle and Hennepin crossed Lake Erie with the first vessel that had ever disturbed the waters of that lake, the face of the country had been, down to the time of the English occupation, but little changed. During the period of the French power in this quarter, the fur-trade had been vigorously carried on along the great chain of lakes, and through every channel in which it could be made to circulate, either by companies chartered for that object, or by individual enterprise. The *coureurs des bois*, who acted, says La Hontan, " like East Indiamen and pirates,"* returning periodically from their inland voyages to swell the population at the different posts, brought with them in bark canoes the furs and peltry which they had collected, and deposited them at the factories erected to receive them: from thence they

* La Hontan's Voyages.

were at regular seasons transported to the head-quarters of the trade at Montreal and Quebec, where they were shipped for Europe.

The principal channels through which this traffic was carried on between the upper and lower provinces, continued to be the Ottawa River or Lake Erie, the packs, when the latter course was adopted, being transported across the portage of Niagara Falls upon the backs of the traders.

The condition of this trade under the French, although depending much on the peculiar character of the people, was essentially modified by the positive operation of the laws. The government of the colony was, it is true, exercised with apparent mildness, but still it was impressed with those harsh principles which characterized the most aristocratic period of the Bourbons. Even the form of land distribution, founded on the *Coutume de Paris*, was extended to the French colonies of the West. Its operation was exceedingly oppressive, and greatly retarded the growth of the settlements. It confined the energies of the people to narrow tracts of land, granted under burdensome conditions, placing them in the power of *seigneurs*, which was but another name for masters, instead of opening the broad and fertile bosom of the West to free and unencumbered industry, such as is now effecting such extraordinary changes in that region under the equal laws of our own republic. The people under this system were but the mere appendages of large corporations, parts of a vast machine which was planned and kept in motion solely for the benefit of royal monopolies.

It has been remarked that the aspect of things in these remote regions was but little changed after they came into the possession of the English. The chapels and the forts continued in much the same state; the little farms of the French, surrounded by pickets, stretched along the banks of the streams as before; and the country presented a variegated aspect of French, English, and Indian manners.* The red coats of the British regulars contrasted very strikingly with the peasant garb of the French farmers, and with the wild and fantastic dress of the natives.

The insurrection being quelled, a system of conciliatory measures was adopted to secure the good-will of the disaffected tribes; small grants of land were made around the posts, and the Indians themselves were induced to cede portions of their territory for a trifling consideration to the French colonists. These grants were made, however, without any authority from the British government. The French settlements extended along the banks of the Detroit and St. Clair Rivers to the distance

* Carver.

of about twenty miles above and below the town, with here and there a lonely hut of some French trader at a favourable point in the interior. Detroit continued to be the most prominent post, and three years after the Pontiac war the town contained not less than a hundred houses, independent of the barracks. On the west side of the town lay the commons, which received the name of the *King's Garden.* The fort was surrounded by pickets and mounted with small cannon, was garrisoned by two hundred men, and the commandant exercised a sort of arbitrary power under the general supervision of the Governor-general of Canada.*

Meanwhile the Hudson's Bay Company, which had been long a rival of the old French companies, extended its operations through the wilderness which had been the ranging ground of the French traders. This company had been chartered in 1669 by Charles II. That charter, granted to a company of English merchants, authorized them to occupy a very extensive region north of Canada for the prosecution of the fur-trade, to establish military posts for the defence of their persons and property, and to traffic with the native tribes.

From 1763 to the close of the three following years, the trade from Montreal with the interior had been greatly diminished, the Indians car-

* Carver.

rying on most of their traffic with the agents of the Hudson's Bay Company. In 1766 individual adventurers began to extend their operations along the lake shores, in the same track that had formerly been pursued by the French, and soon came in collision with the large companies which were striving to occupy for their exclusive benefit this extensive region. Thus the course of the trade continued to present the same wild features which had characterized it under the former *régime.*

The English made but little change either in the laws or in their administration, and pursued the same general policy as had their predecessors the French. The commandants of the posts, although responsible to the governor-general at Quebec, were still possessed of a discretionary power which was all but absolute, and which they exercised in a highly arbitrary manner, as perhaps was necessary among such a population as they had to deal with. Whenever any crime was committed, however, which required a formal trial, it was customary for these officers to summon a jury of the most respectable inhabitants, and to abide by their decision.

A semblance of the criminal laws of England was, it is true, introduced, but these laws were administered without any regard to fixed principles or to established rules. A single example will suffice to show the manner in which legal proceedings were conducted in 1776.

Governor Hamilton, at that time the commanding officer at Detroit, being informed of a theft committed by a Canadian Frenchman, directed Philip Dejean and twelve jurors to hear and adjudge the case: they accordingly proceeded to the trial, and convicted the individual of the crime alleged against him. The record of this trial has come down to us, and it is a most singular document. Lord Dorchester, however, then governor of Canada, was no sooner made acquainted with the proceedings in this case, so contrary to every principle of law, than he issued a warrant for the arrest of Hamilton and Dejean, though, unfortunately, they had both previously left the country.*

In 1774 an act was passed, called the Quebec Act, establishing the boundaries of Canada, including Michigan, and extending thence to the Mississippi and Ohio Rivers on the south, and north from the St. Lawrence to the latitude of 52°, or to the lands of the Hudson's Bay Company. This act granted to the Catholic inhabitants the free exercise of their religion, the undisturbed possession of their Church property, and the right in all matters of litigation to demand a trial according to the former

* Colonial Record of 1776.

laws of the province. But this right was not extended to the settlers on lands granted by the English crown. The criminal laws of England were introduced into Canada, and the crown reserved to itself the right of establishing courts of civil, criminal, and ecclesiastical jurisdiction.*

The enterprise of the people was not wholly confined to the fur-trade. The mineral region upon the shores of Lake Superior had been visited as early as 1773; a project was formed for working the copper ore discovered there, and a company in England had obtained a charter for that object. This company consisted of the Duke of Gloucester, Mr. Secretary Townshend, Sir Samuel Tutchet, Bart., Mr. Baxter, consul of the Empress of Russia, Mr. Cruikshank, Sir William Johnston, Bart., Mr. Bostwick, and Alexander Henry, the French fur-trader who figured so conspicuously in the fall of Michilimackinac. A sloop was accordingly purchased, and the miners commenced their operations. They soon found, however, that the expenses of blasting and of transportation were too great to warrant the prosecution of the enterprise, and it was abandoned. Previous to this, a company of English adventurers had embarked in the same project, but they also gave it up on account, as they said, "of the distracted state of affairs in America."†

* M'Gregor

† Henry.

In 1783 several influential merchants, who had been individually engaged in the fur-trade, entered into partnership for its more vigorous prosecution, though without any charter, and established what was styled the Northwest Company. The stock of this company was divided into sixteen shares. No money was paid in, but each of the partners engaged to furnish his proportion of the goods necessary to carry on the trade.

In 1787 the shareholders appointed from their number special agents to import from England such goods as might be required, and to store them at Montreal. The plan they adopted for conducting the trade was similar to that which had been pursued by the French. The European goods were, by the orders of the agents, made into such articles as were wanted by the traders and Indians, and packed up and forwarded, and the money for the outfits was also supplied by them.*

Storehouses were erected in convenient and accessible situations on the borders of the lakes, and the posts formerly occupied by the French were employed for the same purpose. Connected with these there were also trading-houses, and places where the various persons employed in carrying on the trade might be accommodated. Agents were sent to Detroit, Mackinaw, the Sault de Ste. Marie, and

* M'Kenzie.

the Grand Portage near Lake Superior, where the furs were deposited when brought from the interior, and whose business it was to have them packed and sent to Montreal for shipment to England.*

The most important point of the fur-trade was the Grand Portage of Lake Superior, situated in a remote region to the northwest, where the greatest quantity of furs could be collected. Here the proprietors of the establishment, the guides, clerks, and interpreters, messed together in a large hall hung round with elk-horns, ornamented pipes, hatchets, and other implements used by the Indians in war and peace, while the canoe-men, or *coureurs des bois,* were allowed nothing but a dish which they called "hommony," consisting of Indian corn boiled in a strong alkali and seasoned with fat.

The persons employed in this traffic were a motley and very peculiar race. Besides the clerks, interpreters, and guides, there was a numerous body, half Indian and half French, which had been constantly increasing in this quarter from the frequent intermarriages between the traders and the native women. The canoes employed by them were of large size, each one being capable of containing ten men and about sixty-five packages of furs.

The European goods purchased for this traffic

* M'Kenzie.

consisted of blankets, cutlery, glass beads, and other trinkets, besides different articles that were obtained at Montreal.

These goods were ordered from England the season before they were wanted, shipped from London the following spring, and arrived in Canada early in the summer. Here they were made up into packages of a convenient size, weighing each about ninety pounds, sent to the interior the next spring, exchanged for furs during the succeeding winter, and the following autumn these furs were received at Montreal and shipped for London.*

Thus this interesting trade, which had been carried on for more than a century, still continued to circulate in its ordinary channels along the waters of the lakes. But the spirit of mercantile rivalry was carried to a great extent, and, unhappily, excited all the worst passions in the human breast. The Hudson Bay and Northwest Companies, the respective boundaries of which were not very clearly defined, came into active and desperate collision, and made repeated attacks upon the trading-posts of each other. Lord Selkirk, however, having placed himself at the head of the Hudson's Bay Company, succeeded at length in uniting the stock of the two companies, and thus put an end to the strife. These two companies held dominion

* M'Kenzie.

over the territory bordering on the lakes, and studied only to keep it a barren, howling waste, that they might the better fill their own coffers.

The American Revolution was now about to break forth. The people of the English colonies at the East had declared that they would not submit to be taxed by the mother-country unless they were represented in the British Parliament. A duty having been imposed upon tea, a vessel lying in Boston harbour with a quantity of it on board had been taken possession of by a party of the inhabitants, and the obnoxious article was thrown into the sea. From this may be dated the commencement of a struggle which, in the desperation with which it was fought and the magnitude of its results, is scarcely paralleled in history.

During this eventful struggle, the wilderness then comprising the territory of the present State of Michigan, with but a small population, consisting principally of British soldiers and persons connected with the fur-trade, from its remote situation was but little affected by the war, though the Indians within its borders were employed to harass the American settlements upon the frontiers of New-York, Pennsylvania, and Virginia.

Detroit and Michilimackinac were during this period the points of greatest interest. At these posts the Indian warriors were assembled and furnished with arms and ammunition, and from thence they were despatched against the nearest American settlements, to pillage, burn, and destroy, and to massacre and scalp the defenceless inhabitants. On their return from their murderous expeditions, these savage allies were met by the British commanders in the council-houses of Mackinaw and Detroit, and there received the stipulated price for the scalps which they brought.

It is not to be wondered at that the European inhabitants of Michigan and Canada should have been opposed to the doctrines of the American Revolution. The French population had been accustomed to a despotic government, and from habit were little inclined to any other; while the English colonists were mere adventurers, and had come to the country for no other reason than to benefit their fortunes by its trade. They were therefore actuated by a totally different spirit from that which animated the inhabitants of the original English colonies, who were fixed in their habits, and who had fled from the persecution of the people of England, that they might enjoy, undisturbed, the right of self-government in matters of religion.

Not only were parties of Indians sent out against the American settlements, but in some instances they were supported by the regular troops and the local militia. One of these joint expeditions, commanded by Captain Byrd, set out from Detroit to attack Louisville. It proceeded in boats as far as it could ascend the Maumee River, and from thence crossed over to the Ohio; but the high water here preventing them from reaching the place for which they started, they marched to what is called Ruddle's Station. The formidable force which they presented intimidated the garrison at this post, and it immediately surrendered, under the promise of being protected from the Indians. This promise, however, was violated, and the prisoners were all massacred. A small stockade, called Martin's Station, was likewise taken by the same commander, and his advance threw the whole region into the utmost consternation, when he suddenly withdrew.*

Another expedition started from Detroit under the command of Henry Hamilton, the commandant of the post. At that time the feeble settlements in what now comprises Kentucky were much exposed to the hostile inroads of the savages, and General Clarke, an officer of great bravery and experience, had been sent by the governor of Virginia for their defence. Supposing that he could the better accomplish his object by reducing Kaskaskia, Kahokia, and other small French settlements in this region, which were believed to be friendly to the

* Cass.

British cause, he descended the river and took possession of them.

Governor Hamilton was no sooner informed of these proceedings than he collected a force of regulars, militia, and Indians, and proceeded to St. Vincent, where he halted to make arrangements for active operations as soon as the season would permit. His design was to recover the posts which had been captured by General Clarke, to attack and defeat the force under his command, and destroy the infant settlements of the Americans in this region.

General Clarke was soon advised of the movements of Hamilton. A Spanish merchant informed him that this officer was extremely careless in his operations, and that he had sent a part of his force to the Ohio River to destroy the settlements along its banks. The American general accordingly despatched an armed boat to the Wabash, with orders to her commander not to permit anything to pass that river, while he himself set out with one hundred and thirty men for the same point, although in the depth of winter. Sixteen days were occupied in crossing the country, the soldiers sometimes marching up to their breasts in water along the shores of the Wabash, that stream having overflowed its banks. As soon as they arrived at St. Vincent, the soldiers were drawn up in order of battle, and, with the trunk of a tree formed in the shape of a cannon, they boldly advanced to attack the British post. Governor Hamilton, supposing that he was about to be assailed by artillery, immediately surrendered. The British were suffered to return to Detroit; but their commander, who was known to have been active in instigating the Indians to commit the greatest barbarities, was placed in irons, and sent to Virginia as a prisoner of war.*

Still some of the savages were not well affected to the British cause. As early as in 1776, the Delawares had received a message from the Hurons of Detroit, requesting them to "*keep their shoes in readiness* to unite with their warriors." Netawatwees, however, the chief of the Delawares, who wished to remain neutral, would not listen to this proposal, but sent to the Huron chief in return several belts of wampum, admonishing him at the same time to keep quiet, and to remember the misery which the Hurons had formerly brought upon themselves by engaging in wars on the side of the French. The reply of the Delawares was delivered in the presence of De Peyster, the English commandant, who cut the belts of wampum in pieces, threw them on the ground, and commanded the messengers who brought them instantly to quit the country.†

* Cass. † Loskiel.

Certain Moravian missionaries, who were engaged in their peaceful and pious labours on the banks of the Muskingum, did not escape the suspicions of the English in this quarter. These disinterested and charitable men were accused of holding a secret correspondence with the Congress at Philadelphia, and of contributing their influence, as well as that of their Indian congregation, to aid the American cause.

The Indian agent was therefore sent to Niagara, and a grand council of the Iroquois was assembled, at which those tribes were urged to break up the Indian congregation collected by the Moravians. Not wishing, however, to have anything to do with it, they sent a message to the Chippewas and Ottawas, with a belt, stating that they gave the Indian congregation into their hands "to make soup of."*

In 1781 the Moravian missionaries arrived at Detroit, where they were immediately brought before De Peyster, the English commandant. A war council was held at the same time, when the council-house was completely filled, the different tribes being arranged on either side. The assembly was addressed in a long speech by Captain Pipe, the principal chief of the Wolf tribe, who had committed the most savage barbarities upon the scattered American settlements. He told the com-

* Loskiel.

mandant "that the English might fight the Americans if they chose: it was their cause, and not his; that they had raised a quarrel among themselves, and that it was their business to fight it out. They had set him on the Americans," he said, "as the hunter sets his dog upon the game." By the side of the British commander stood a war-chief, with a stick in his hand four feet in length, strung with American scalps. "Now, father," said he, presenting the stick and addressing himself to the commandant, "here is what has been done with the hatchet you gave me. I have made the use of it that you ordered me to do, and found it sharp."*

It was by such influences that these savage tribes were instigated to commit the most atrocious cruelties against the defenceless American settlements on the frontiers during the whole course of the Revolutionary war. Every avenue was closed whereby a different influence might be introduced among them, and they were made to believe that the Americans were only seeking to possess themselves of their lands, and to drive them away from the territory they had inherited from their forefathers.

But, after the country from Maine to Florida had been drenched with blood in this great contest

* Loskiel.

for freedom, the American cause was at last triumphant; and by the treaty of peace concluded at Versailles in 1783, an end was at least temporarily put to these barbarities: the distant settlers were permitted once more to resume their labours, and to sleep without alarm.

CHAPTER VII.

Northwestern Territory organized.—Arthur St. Clair appointed Governor.—English refuse to surrender the Posts.—Indian Disaffection.—Indian Council at Detroit.—Message from the Spanish Settlements on the Banks of the Mississippi.—Campaign of General Harmar.—Campaign of General St. Clair.—Campaign of General Wayne.—Extension of French Settlements.—Michigan surrendered to the United States.—Condition of the Territory in connexion with the Fur-trade.—Currency employed in the Fur-trade.

But, although the war was at an end, the posts and trading stations along the lakes, within the acknowledged limits of the United States, were not given up. Of the real causes which induced the British government, in violation of all the principles of good faith, to retain these posts, we have no means of judging. It may, however, be fairly inferred from the conduct of individuals, that if that government did not actually and by direct means promote the Indian war which broke out at this time, it did not, to say the least, discountenance it.

There is ample evidence to show that British emissaries were sent to the remote Indian tribes on the borders of the lakes to instigate them to take up arms, and that, after they had done so, they looked for aid from the English garrisons within the American territory. In the treaty of peace of 1783, there was no express stipulation in regard to the surrender of the northwestern posts; but by the second article of Jay's treaty in 1794, it was agreed that the British troops should be withdrawn from all the posts assigned to the United States by the former treaty (of 1783) on or before the first day of June, 1796.

The conduct of England in so long persisting in retaining possession of a country which did not belong to her, we shall not pretend to account for; but the value of this country, from the richness of its soil and its other advantages, soon began to attract attention.

Measures were accordingly taken for its temporary government. The circumstance which had more particularly directed the public attention to this western domain was a memorial from the soldiers and officers of the Revolutionary army, presented to General Washington in 1783, setting forth their claims to a portion of the public lands. Nothing, however, was granted to them at that time.*

The country had been completely exhausted by the terrible struggle in which it had been so long

* North American Review.

engaged, and, heavily burdened with debt, it was now seeking for some means by which it could secure its liquidation; and as the war had been prosecuted for the general good, it was held that the states claiming lands in this quarter were bound to grant portions of them for this object. The territory northwest of the Ohio was claimed by several of the Eastern States, on the ground that it was included within the limits indicated by their charters from the English crown. In answer to the wishes of the government and people, these states in a patriotic spirit surrendered their claims to this extensive territory, that it might constitute a common fund to aid in the payment of the national debt.

To prepare the way for this cession, a law had been passed in October, 1780, that the territory so to be ceded should be disposed of for the common benefit of the whole Union; that the states erected therein should be of suitable extent, not less than one hundred nor more than one hundred and fifty miles square; and that any expenses that might be incurred in recovering the posts then in the hands of the British should be reimbursed.

New-York released her claims to Congress on the 1st of March, 1781; Virginia on the 1st of the same month, 1784; Massachusetts on the 19th of April, 1785; and Connecticut on the 4th of September, 1786.

Meanwhile, the Iroquois in 1784 conveyed to the United States all their right to any lands west of Pennsylvania; and on the 1st of January, 1785, by the treaty of Fort M'Intosh, the Ottawas, Chippewas, Delawares, and Wyandots surrendered all the lands claimed by them south of the Ohio, a belt of territory six miles broad, commencing at the River Raisin and extending along the strait to Lake St. Clair, a tract of twelve miles square at the Rapids of the Maumee, together with the Islands of Bois Blanc and Mackinaw, and also a tract six miles by three on the mainland, to the north of the last-mentioned island. These different cessions having been obtained from the native tribes, in 1787 a government was organized for this extensive region, which received the name of the *North-west Territory.**

It is unnecessary here to examine particularly the details of this ordinance: it was based on the principles of civil liberty maintained in the Magna Charta of England, re-enacted in the bill of rights, and incorporated into our different state constitutions. This ordinance, it is well known, was drawn up by Nathan Dane, of Beverley, Massachusetts, a benevolent and excellent man, and a distinguished lawyer, who was the compiler of a very valuable abridgment of American Law, and

* North American Review.

the founder of the Dane Law school in the University of Cambridge.

On the 7th of April, 1788, a company of forty-seven individuals landed at the spot where Marietta now stands, and there commenced the settlement of Ohio. The first code of laws for this territory was published by nailing them to the body of a tree upon the banks of the Muskingum, and Return Jonathan Meigs was appointed to administer them, the governor, Arthur St. Clair, not having yet arrived.

We have seen that the Western posts were still retained by the British government, notwithstanding the peace concluded in 1783. Several questions of no little interest had sprung up, which excited unfriendly feelings between the two nations, and governed their policy. Debts due by Americans to British subjects, the payment of which had been guarantied by the treaty, were not paid; and on the other hand, the slaves belonging to American citizens, and who had been taken away by the British officers, were not restored. In consequence of this unsettled state of things, when the Baron Steuben was sent by General Washington to Sir Frederic Haldimand at Quebec to arrange matters for the occupation of these posts, with instructions to proceed to Michigan, and along the line of the lake frontier, for the purpose of taking possession of them, he was informed that they would not be given up, and was refused passports to Niagara and Detroit.*

Combined with the retention of the posts, a new confederacy among the savages was evidently organizing in the West. As early as December, 1786, a grand council of the different tribes was held near the mouth of the Detroit River. At this council were delegates from the Six Nations, from the Hurons, the Ottawas, the Miamis, the Shawanese, the Chippewas, the Cherokees, the Delawares, the Pottawatamies, and from the confederates of the Wabash. The principal subject of discussion at this council appears to have been a question of boundary. It was contended by the Indians that the United States had no right to cross the Ohio River, but they advised a pacific line of policy so long as there was no actual encroachment upon their territory. The design of this discussion undoubtedly was to create a belief that the Americans intended to drive them from their lands, and, as was said, to "kindle their council fires wherever they thought proper, without consulting the Indians." The American government, indeed, considered that the treaty of 1783 vested in them jurisdiction over the Indian territory: a claim which the native occupants were by no means disposed to admit. At this time, also, the United States

* Stone

were at issue with a foreign power respecting the right of navigating the Mississippi.

Among other things, as a plea for still retaining the Western posts, it was pretended by the English that the extensive and valuable country in which they were situated had been ceded away through some oversight on the part of the commissioners, or from their ignorance of the geography of the country. But the real motives by which they were actuated are sufficiently manifest. They had already succeeded in exciting hostile feelings among the Indian tribes, and this they were determined to take advantage of for the purpose of preventing this broad and fertile region from passing out of their hands.

Many of the half-breeds were also active in seconding the views of the English, not only by inflaming the minds of the Indians, but by promising to take up arms in their cause, from a belief that if they did not thus side with them, they would not afterward be suffered to trade in their territory. Meanwhile, Alexander M'Kenzie, an agent of the British government, visited Detroit, painted like a savage, and stated that he had just returned from the remote tribes of the upper lakes, who were all in arms, and prepared to oppose the claims of the Americans to the western lands; that large bodies of warriors had already assembled, and that they were about to attack the infant settlements of Virginia and Ohio.* The artifice practised by M'Kenzie succeeded to his wish; and he could the better operate upon the prejudices and passions of the Indians, as he spoke their language perfectly well. Elliot and the notorious Simon Girty were no less active in exciting the savages to war.

In 1794 an agent was sent from the Spanish settlements on the banks of the Mississippi for the same object, and to hasten the organization of the Indian confederacy against the United States. "Children," said he to his savage auditors, "you see me on my feet, grasping the tomahawk to strike them (the Americans). We will strike together. I do not desire you to go before me in the front, but to follow me. Children, you hear what these distant nations have said to us, so that we have nothing to do but to put our designs into immediate execution, and to forward this pipe to the three warlike nations who have been so long struggling for their country. Tell them to smoke this pipe, and to forward it to all the lake Indians, and to their Northern brethren. Then nothing will be wanting to complete our general union from the rising to the setting of the sun, and all the nations will be ready to add strength to the blow we are going to strike."† Excited by these

* Schoolcraft † Stone.

various means, bands of savage warriors, armed with the tomahawk and scalping-knife, were seen hastening towards the lake posts, and another great Indian confederacy was formed, consisting of the Ottawas, the Pottawatamies, the Wyandots, the Miamis, the Chippewas, and the Delawares.

As early as 1785 and 1786, the hostile Indians had occasionally sent their war-parties against the feeble frontier settlements in Kentucky and along the banks of the Ohio, where a few enterprising emigrants from Virginia and New-England had erected their little clusters of log cabins.

These border incursions, which most clearly appear to have been countenanced by the British, induced the American government in 1790 to send into that quarter General Josiah Harmar, an accomplished and able officer, to put a stop to them. He advanced against the hostile tribes with a force amounting to fourteen hundred men; but, imprudently dividing his army, he was taken by surprise, and defeated by a body of Indians led on by that sanguinary and desperate warrior, the Little Turtle.*

General Harmar, having failed in his enterprise, was succeeded by Major-general St. Clair, the governor of the Northwestern Territory; and in October, 1792, this officer advanced into the Indian country with a force of about two thousand men.

* Stone.

Warned as he was by the disaster that had proved so fatal to his predecessor, he fell into an ambuscade that had been laid for him, where the Indians, firing from behind their breastwork of fallen trees, carried destruction into the American ranks, and soon covered the ground with their dead. So sudden and unexpected was the attack, and so murderous the fire of the enemy, that the general was compelled to order a retreat, leaving his artillery in the hands of the savages.

On account of these repeated disasters, it became necessary to increase the army by enlistments, and to push a still stronger force against the hostile Indian tribes. General Washington therefore made the most strenuous efforts to effect this object; but, owing to the panic produced by the disastrous defeats of Harmar and St. Clair, with but little success. There was, moreover, no small opposition to the war; and additional measures were deemed necessary to bring it to a close.

In 1793 General St. Slair was succeeded by General Anthony Wayne in the command of the Western army. Advancing through the forest to the spot which had been rendered memorable by the defeat of St. Clair, he there constructed a fort upon the site of the old fortification, and called it Fort Recovery.* Situated in the midst of the

* Stone.

scene of former carnage, there might then have been seen around it, under the trees and amid the fallen logs, the bleached bones of those who had been slain.

General Wayne soon reached the confluence of the Au Glaize and Maumee Rivers, and found the villages spread along the bottoms of the latter completely deserted. A short time afterward he arrived at the Rapids of the Maumee, and erected there a fort about four miles above the British post, which he called Fort Deposite, in which he placed his stores and baggage. This British post, established on American ground, had been fortified by a detachment sent from Detroit the preceding spring, and the Indians appeared to look upon it as their last refuge in case they were attacked.

The British government had demanded, before the treaty of 1783, as one of the conditions of peace, the complete independence of the savage tribes, with, of course, the power to grant their lands to whomsoever they pleased.* The Americans having refused to accede to this condition, that post was established on the banks of the Miami for the purpose, it was believed, of countenancing the Indians, and of actively supporting them should they gain the ascendancy. General Wayne therefore felt it necessary to advance with the utmost

* Thatcher.

caution, as everything depended not only upon his courage, but his prudence. He had been directed, however, in case he was opposed by the British, to treat them according to the usages of war.

The American commander was not long in coming up with his savage foe. The Indians regarded him with great fear from his supposed cunning, calling him the *Blacksnake* on that account; while the American army, consisting of three thousand men, no doubt presented a truly formidable appearance to them.

The Indian force, their whole strength being collected at this point, was in point of numbers about the same. Most of the savages were naked, and painted for battle. Stationed in a dense forest, and protected by the rocky bank of the river and a breastwork of fallen trees, they were disposed in three lines within supporting distance of each other.

Wayne's *Legion* consisted of two thousand regulars and one thousand mounted militia, under General Scott, of Kentucky. The right flank of his army rested on the river, a brigade of mounted volunteers under General Todd occupied the left, and General Babee, with his division, formed the rear. Major Price was ordered to advance with a select battalion of riflemen and reconnoitre, and, if attacked, to retreat in pretended confusion, in order to entice the enemy towards the main body. The stratagem proved successful; and while the savages were rushing forward and startling the wilderness with their yells of triumph, the American army advanced against them with trailed arms, being ordered to press them with the bayonet, to rouse them from their lurking-places, and deliver a close fire upon their backs, so as to allow them no opportunity to escape. The Indians now began to break, and retreated towards the walls of Fort Maumee. While these events were taking place, the gates of the fort had been shut, and the English within gazed with apparent indifference upon the scene. In the action there was actually engaged on the side of the savages a force from Detroit, headed by a prominent individual of that place. General Wayne destroyed the Indian villages and the corn-fields on the banks of the Maumee, and proceeded towards Fort Defiance.*

Before he left the battle-ground, however, he paraded his force in front of the British post, that they might see its strength, while he advanced with his staff towards the glacis to examine the character of the position, and to ascertain, as far as was possible, what were the intentions of the garrison. The American officers, as they drew near, could discover the British soldiers, with matches lighted and standing by their guns, ready for any emer-

* Stone.

gency that might arise. Some attempts were made by his officers to persuade the British commander to revenge this insulting parade before his post by allowing them to salute the Americans with a discharge from their artillery. Nothing of this kind, however, was permitted, though a correspondence of no very friendly character took place. General Wayne finally succeeded in concluding a treaty with the Indians at Greenville, which effectually broke up the confederacy.*

The settlements in Michigan up to this period had advanced but slowly. The French Canadians had extended their farms to a considerable distance along the banks of the St. Clair; and on the Detroit River there were a few straggling French settlements, as also on Otter Creek, and on the rivers Rouge, Pointe aux Tremblé, and other small streams flowing into Lake Erie. Agriculture and the fur-trade constituted nearly the entire occupation of the inhabitants.

Detroit and Frenchtown, both in the eastern part of the peninsula, were at this time the only places of much importance. The former was merely a small cluster of rude wooden houses, defended by a fort, and surrounded by pickets, and formed, as it had long done, the principal depôt for the fur-trade. The population, independent of the soldiers of the

* See Appendix E.

garrison, consisted principally of Scotch, French, and English merchants, who had removed here after the conquest of the country, for the prosecution of that traffic. The goods required here were obtained from Montreal, and bills of credit for small sums, payable at that place or at Quebec, were allowed to be issued by the merchants, on condition of their giving security to double their amount. Frenchtown, on the River Raisin, now a place of considerable importance, consisted at that time of only a few log cabins, erected by the French on either bank of the river. Two Indian villages, one occupied by the Ottawas, the other by the Pottawatamies, stood on the present site of the City of Monroe. Being a depôt for the Northwestern Company, the surrounding Indians periodically resorted there to exchange their furs and peltry for cloths, beads, silver ornaments, firearms, ammunition, and such other articles as they required. The French settlers in the vicinity also disposed of their corn here in exchange for goods, and from thence it was transported to the upper lakes for the use of the traders.*

About this time a project was started, which, had it been successful, would have been highly injurious to the interests of this part of the West. In 1795, Robert Randall, of Pennsylvania, and Charles

* Manuscripts from Detroit.

Whitney, of Vermont, in connexion with several merchants of Detroit, entered into a compact, the object of which was to appropriate to themselves a tract of territory comprising nearly twenty millions of acres, situated between Lakes Erie, Huron, and Michigan.* This was to be done by securing to themselves the pre-emption right. The land was to be divided into forty-one shares, five of which were to be apportioned among the traders of Detroit who were parties to the agreement, six were to be given to Randall and those associated with him, and the remainder were to be distributed among members of Congress who should exert their influence in procuring the passage of the necessary law. The amount proposed to be paid for this vast tract was from half a million to a million of dollars; and it was believed that the merchants of Detroit had sufficient influence with the Indians to induce them to part with the land. In opposition to the measure, it was represented that, under the treaty of 1783, the right of purchase belonged exclusively to the United States; while, on the other hand, it was urged that the Indians were dissatisfied with this treaty, and did not consider themselves bound by it, and that the plan proposed would alone establish tranquillity among them, and secure peace to the country. But, as soon as the corrupt char-

* Biddle's Discourse.

acter of the plan was discovered, the two principal projectors were brought before the bar of the House of Representatives, when, on the hearing of the evidence, Randall was discharged, but Whitney was fined to the amount of the costs which had accrued, and received a severe reprimand.*

The Indian power having been broken by Wayne's victory, and the treaty of Greenville binding the savages from farther aggression, the island of Mackinaw was at last surrendered, and Detroit also given up, the retiring garrison, to show their spite, locking the gates of the fort, breaking the windows in the barracks, and filling the wells with stones, in order to annoy the new occupants as much as was in their power. The latter post was soon after taken possession of by a detachment of troops under the command of Captain Porter, and the American flag hoisted on its ramparts for the first time. Thus Michigan at last passed quietly into the possession of the United States.

While the English held this country, Mackinaw was the chief place of rendezvous for the Indians and the traders of the Northwest Company. Starting from this picturesque island in huge canoes, propelled by the *voyageurs*, the merchants would at times sweep across the sparkling waters of those inland seas, provided with the means of the most

* Biddle's Discourse.

luxurious revelry, and, encamping on their shores, would there hold their feasts, surrounded by half-bred dependants, traders, and Indians.

While the French were in possession of this country, as there was but little coin for general circulation, accounts were kept in beaver-skins or other furs reduced to their current value. The price of beaver at Michilimackinac in 1765 was two shillings and sixpence the pound, Michilimackinac currency; otter-skins were six shillings each, and martin-skins one shilling and sixpence. Ten beaver-skins were given for a stroud blanket, eight for a white blanket, two for a pound of powder, one for a pound of shot or ball, twenty for a gun, two for an axe of one pound weight, and one for a knife. The notes and coin of Quebec were sometimes seen at the lake posts, but not in sufficient quantity to be relied on for a uniform currency.

CHAPTER VIII.

Condition of Michigan after the Surrender of the Posts.—Its Erection into a Territory.—General Hull appointed Governor. —Detroit destroyed by Fire.—Administration of the Law.—Third Indian Confederacy under Tecumseh and the Prophet. —Le Marquoit.—Land-office established.—Walk-in-the-Water.—Population in 1811.—Memorial from Michigan praying Aid from the General Government.—Savage Outbreak.—Operations on the Wabash.—American Fur Company.

It was a long time after this fertile but uncultivated territory came into the possession of the United States before its character was materially changed. The Canadian French continued to form the principal part of its population. The interior of the country was but little known except by the Indians and the traders, who explored it in the pursuit of furs. As the effect of transferring the jurisdiction from France to England had been little more than to change the garrisons from French to English, and to give to the Hudson's Bay Company a monopoly of the fur-trade, so its surrender to the United States produced but little alteration in its general features. As the Indian title was not fully extinguished, no lands were brought into market, and, consequently, the settlements proceeded but very slowly.

In the division of the Northwestern Territory, what is now the State of Michigan constituted a single county, which received the name of Wayne. It sent one representative to the Legislature of the Northwestern Territory, which was held at Chilicothe. A Court of Common Pleas was organized for the county, and the General Court of the whole territory sometimes met at Detroit. No roads had as yet been constructed through the interior, nor were there any settlements except on the frontiers. The habits of the people were essentially military, and but little attention was paid to agriculture except by the French peasantry. In winter they drove their carrioles over the ice with their Canadian ponies, that were of Norman stock, many of which are now to be seen in this country; and in summer they employed small wooden carts, well adapted to the state of the roads, for the carriage of their goods—vehicles that are still used.

The state continued to send a representative to the General Assembly of the Northwestern Territory at Chilicothe until 1800, when Indiana was erected into a separate territory; and two years afterward it was annexed to this new-formed territory, and remained under its jurisdiction until 1805. In the month of January of that year it was erected into a separate territory, and William Hull was appointed the first governor The system of government was somewhat peculiar, the executive power being confided in the governor, the judicial in three judges, who were authorized to "adopt and publish" laws suited to the territory, and not incompatible with the ordinance of 1787, and the legislative power was exercised by the two jointly. On the 25th of July of that year the territory was divided into three districts, namely, Erie, Huron, and Michilimackinac, for each of which a court was established, to be held by one of the judges of the Supreme Court of the territory, with exclusive jurisdiction in criminal matters, and also in all civil cases above the sum of twenty dollars, those below this sum being cognizable by justices of the peace. A few years afterward it was divided into counties, in each of which was organized a County Court.* The laws thus introduced were, as might be expected, crude and ill digested, as is abundantly attested by the records of the courts at that period, which are still preserved.

General Hull, when he arrived at Detroit to assume his official duties as governor of the territory, found the town in ruins, it having been destroyed by fire.† Whether this disaster had been occasioned by accident or design was not known. However this may have been, as the town was very compact, covering only two acres of ground,

* Territorial Laws. † Biddle's Discourse.

and the materials were of the most combustible nature, it was soon entirely consumed, and the unfortunate inhabitants were obliged to encamp in the open fields, almost destitute of food and shelter. Still they were not discouraged, and soon commenced rebuilding their houses on the same site. The General Government also took their case into consideration, and an act of Congress was passed, granting to the sufferers the site of the old town of Detroit, and ten thousand acres of land adjoining it.

A judiciary system was now established, and the territorial militia were organized. In October of the same year a report was made to Congress of the condition of the territory, and in May of the following year a code of laws was adopted similar to those of the original states. This code was signed by Governor Hull, Augustus B. Woodward and Frederic Bates, judges of the territory, and was called the "Woodward Code." The bounds of the territorial government, as then established, embraced all the country on the American side of the Detroit River, east of a north and south line drawn through the centre of Lake Michigan.

The Indian land-claims had been partially extinguished previous to this period. By the treaty of Fort M'Intosh in 1785, and that of Fort Harmar in 1787, extensive cessions had either been made or confirmed, and in the year 1807 the Indian titles to several tracts became entirely extinct.

In consequence of the settlements which had been made under the French and English governments, some confusion sprang up in regard to the titles to valuable tracts that were claimed by different individuals under the French laws. Congress accordingly passed an act establishing a board of commissioners to examine and settle these conflicting claims; and in 1807 another act was passed, confirming to a certain extent the titles of all such as had been in possession of the lands then occupied by them from the year 1796, when the territory was surrendered, up to the date of that act. Other acts were subsequently passed, extending the same conditions to the settlements on the upper lakes.*

In addition to their settlements along the shores of the Detroit and St. Clair Rivers, and the lake of the latter name, where there was a continued line of cottages, with farms adjoining, containing orchards of pear and apple trees, planted, probably, in the reign of Louis XIV., and the old posts on the island of Mackinaw, at Ste. Marie and at St. Joseph, the French colonists had a line of cabins on the River Raisin, where the city of Monroe (then called Frenchtown) now stands. The interior of the country was but little known except by those who

* Biddle's Discourse.

were engaged in the fur-trade, and these were interested in representing it in as unfavourable a light as possible. The Indian titles to the land had been but partially extinguished, and no portion of the public domain had been yet brought into market. But few American settlers had therefore ventured into this region, though the adjoining State of Ohio had already acquired a considerable population.*

The distance of this territory also, and the unsettled state of affairs along the western borders of the lakes, necessarily prevented immigration. On the opposite shore there was a jealous foreign power, and the interior of the country was occupied by different savage tribes. The territory, too, had but just emerged from an Indian war, and another was evidently preparing. This third Indian confederacy was not only countenanced by the English, but directly instigated by them. The motives which led to it, and the means resorted to to bring it about, were the same as had proved successful in exciting the former insurrections under Pontiac and the Little Turtle. The old story was revived, that the Americans were about to drive the Indians from their lands that they might occupy them themselves. The chief projectors of this savage league were Tecumseh and his brother the Prophet.

* Biddle's Discourse.

The warlike leader of the enterprise was Tecumseh, while the Prophet, whose Indian name was Elkswatawa, was to operate on the minds of the savages by means of superstition, and to excite in them a spirit of fanaticism still more to inflame their natural ferocity.

The disaffection of these tribes was certainly what might have been expected. They saw a new power encroaching upon the inheritance that had been handed down to them from their ancestors, introducing their hated cultivation upon their soil, and rudely disturbing the graves of their dead. It was not difficult, therefore, to unite them in one last desperate struggle to resist this aggressive and threatening power.

Their titles had been only very partially extinguished, and they complained that, where this had been done, the treaties had been unfairly conducted; that the Indians had been deceived; that they were in a state of intoxication at the time they signed away their lands, and that, even under these circumstances, only a part of the tribes had given their consent. The dissatisfaction thus existing among them was artfully fomented by the agents of the Northwest Company, who foresaw that if the Americans were permitted to occupy this country they would be cut off from a valuable portion of their trade; while the English government, which had ceded away this extensive tract without any very definite notions of its importance or extent, looked with complacency on any attempts made by the savages to retain it in their hands. An overreaching spirit had doubtless actuated many of the pioneer settlers of the West, and wrongs had been inflicted upon the Indians which required correction. Taking advantage of this, the traders, and the English generally, were indefatigable in sowing the seeds of discontent among the savage tribes; and it was contended that they should hold the undisturbed possession of the Northwestern Territory, without surrendering the right of pre-emption to the United States.

The Prophet commenced his mission among the tribes in 1806. Taking advantage of the superstitious notions of the Indians, he told them that the Great Spirit had appeared to him in a dream, and appointed him his agent upon the earth; and that, as such, his own tribe, the Shawanese, being the oldest tribe of the West, he was commanded to direct them to form a general confederacy against the United States. He had been instructed also, he said, to proclaim to the red men that it was the will of the Great Spirit that they should throw away the arts of civilization, return to their skins for clothing, and to their bows and war-clubs for arms, renounce the intoxicating drinks of the white men for pure water, and, in a word, resume all the customs of their ancestors. The Americans, he said, had driven the Indians from the seacoast, and were now preparing to push them into the lakes, so that they had no alternative but to make a stand where they were, and drive back these insatiable intruders to the other side of the Alleghany Mountains.

The plan of this league was in many respects similar to that formed by Pontiac. Tecumseh's intention was to surprise the posts of Detroit, Fort Wayne, Chicago, St. Louis, and Vincennes, and to unite all the tribes from the borders of New-York to the banks of the Mississippi.

As early as the year 1807, the Shawanese chief and his brother the Prophet were actively engaged in sending their emissaries, with presents and war-belts, to the most distant tribes, to induce them to join in the confederacy; and when the comet appeared in 1811, the latter artfully turned it to account, by practising on the superstitions of the savages.* Thus the fame and the influence of the Prophet spread rapidly among the tribes of the Northwest.

On the 4th of May, a special mission, consisting of deputies from the Ottawas, was sent to a distant post upon the borders of Lake Superior, and a

* Drake.

grand council being there assembled, it was addressed by Le Marquoit, or the Trout. He told the Indians that he had been sent by the messenger and representative of the Great Spirit, and that he was commissioned to deliver to them a speech from the " first man whom God had created, said to be in the Shawanese country."*

He then informed them what were the instructions of the Great Spirit in the succeeding address: "I am the father of the English, of the French, of the Spaniards, and of the Indians. I created the first man, who was the common father of all these people as well as of yourselves, and it is through him, whom I have awaked from his long sleep, that I now address you. But the Americans I did not make. They are not my children, but the children of the Evil Spirit. They grew from the scum of the great water when it was troubled by the Evil Spirit, and the froth was driven into the woods by a strong east wind. They are numerous, but I hate them. My children, you must not speak of this talk to the whites; it must be hidden from them. I am now on the earth, sent by the Great Spirit to instruct you. Each village must send me two or more principal chiefs, to represent you, that you may be taught. The bearer of this talk must point out to you the path to my wigwam. I could not

* American State Papers.

come myself to L'Arbre Croche, because the world is changed from what it was. It is broken and leans down, and as it declines the Chippewas and all beyond will fall off and die; therefore you must come to see me and be instructed. Those villages which do not listen to this talk will be cut off from the face of the earth."*

It was by such means that the savages were roused to attack the frontier settlements of the West, and afterward to unite with the English in their war with the United States.

In consequence of these menacing movements of the Indians, it was considered advisable to construct a stockade around the town of Detroit for its defence. The population was as yet small. There had been, indeed, up to that time but little to encourage the settlement of the country. The land had not been offered for sale, and a great portion of Western New-York was still unoccupied: not a single steamer navigated the lakes, nor had any roads been made into the interior.

Nor was the neighbourhood of Detroit without symptoms of Indian disaffection. In September, 1809, a special council of the Hurons was called, near Brownstown, and, at the instigation of their principal chief, Walk-in-the-Water, they freely spoke of their grievances to Governor Hull. The

* American State Papers.

speech addressed by this chief to the governor, setting forth the title of his tribe to a large tract of territory near the mouth of the Detroit River, which was claimed by the United States under the treaty of Greenville, shows how much dissatisfied they were with this treaty, and with the encroachments of the Americans upon their soil. In the midst of all these evidences of discontent on the part of the Indians, Michigan remained in a comparatively defenceless state. There were at this time in the whole territory but nine settlements of any importance; nor was the character of the population at these points such that it could be expected to oppose any very active resistance in the conflict which seemed to be approaching.

These settlements were situated on the Rivers Miami and Raisin, on the Huron of Lake Erie, on the Ecorce, Rouge, and Detroit Rivers, on the Huron of St. Clair, the St. Clair River, and the island of Mackinaw; and, in addition to these, there was here and there a group of huts belonging to the French fur-traders. The villages upon the Maumee, the Raisin, and the Huron of Lake Erie contained a population of about thirteen hundred; the post of Detroit, and the settlements on the Rivers Rouge and Ecorce, and on the Huron of St. Clair, numbered two thousand two hundred; the island of Mackinaw, with the small detached log-houses, about a thousand: Detroit was garrisoned by ninety-four men, and Mackinaw by seventy-nine. Thus the entire population of the state was only about four thousand eight hundred, four fifths of whom were Canadian French, and the remainder chiefly Americans, with a few English and Scotch.*

As there was no longer any doubt of the hostile intentions of the savages, it was deemed prudent to present a memorial to Congress, setting forth the defenceless condition of the territory, and praying for aid from that body. Accordingly, on the 27th of December, 1811, such a petition was drawn up, signed by the principal inhabitants of Detroit, and forwarded to Washington.

The joint efforts of Tecumseh and the Prophet were successful in drawing a large body of Indians, probably not less than eight hundred, from the shores of Lake Superior to the station of the latter at Tippecanoe, though it is supposed that one third of their number died of want and hardship on the way.† Their plans were now nearly ripe for action, and parties of the Ottawas, the Miamis, the Chippewas, the Wyandots, the Mississagies, the Shawanese, and the Winnebagoes were to be seen with their bodies painted for war, and again seizing the hatchet.

The first hostile demonstrations were made

* American State Papers. † Schoolcraft.

against the French settlements, where bands of savage warriors made their appearance, armed for battle, and painted in the most hideous manner, with feathers stuck in their hair, and strings of bears' claws about their necks, entering the houses by force, taking whatever they chose, and wantonly destroying with their tomahawks the beehives in the gardens of the settlers. Near the banks of the Kalamazoo, in the county of the same name, a smith's forge had been set up, where hatchets and knives were made for the approaching contest; and at no great distance from it, in a retired spot, surrounded by a dense forest, the Indian women, with their children, had collected, for the purpose of raising corn to furnish a supply of food for the warriors.

Still more flagrant acts of aggression were perpetrated in the State of Indiana, where numerous murders were committed, and horses and other property stolen. It had been for some time noticed that the savages were collecting about the Prophet's station, apparently with no friendly design. A conference was therefore held, in which it was insisted that these hordes should be made to return to their homes, that the property which had been stolen from the Americans should be restored, and that the murderers should be given up.

Tecumseh, on his part, denied that any league,

such as was complained of, had been formed, and protested that he and his brother had no other object in collecting the tribes together but to strengthen the amicable relations between them, and to improve their moral condition. In regard to the murderers of the whites, who were alleged to have taken refuge among his tribe, he denied that they were there, saying, at the same time, that even if they were, they ought to be forgiven, as he had forgiven the whites who had murdered his own people in Illinois.*

All their plans having been fully matured, the contest at length began in earnest, on the banks of the Wabash, at the Prophet's town ; and, while the battle was raging, the Prophet was seen on an adjoining eminence, singing a war-song, to inflame with greater desperation the savage combatants. It was now no longer doubtful that another fierce and obstinate struggle was to be encountered. The Indian warriors, excited by fanaticism and a thirst for blood, in opposition to their chiefs, hastened from all sides towards the lake frontier to join Tecumseh. Meanwhile, the English on the opposite shores were looking with no small interest upon what was passing, regarding the savages as important allies to their own cause in the conflict in which they expected shortly to be engaged.

* Thatcher.

"My son," said one of their agents to an Indian chief, "keep your eyes fixed on me. My tomahawk is now up; be you ready, but do not strike till I give the signal."*

The statement of the fact should not be omitted, that about this time the American Fur Company was formed, under the auspices of Mr. John Jacob Astor, of New-York. Its operations were carried on much after the manner of the old French and English companies, by establishing chains of posts along the lake shores. This company is still in existence, and annually collects a great quantity of furs, which are sent by the way of the Mississippi or the lakes to New-York, from whence a large part of them are exported to foreign countries. This company has also an extensive fishery on Lake Superior, where they take great quantities of trout and whitefish, which are salted, packed in barrels, and sent to the different ports of the adjoining country.†

* Dawson.

† Irving's Astoria.

CHAPTER IX.

War declared between Great Britain and the United States.—Representations of Governor Hull.—Appointed to Command the Western Army.—Crosses to Sandwich and Addresses the Canadians.—Policy of Prevost.—Surrender of Detroit.—Tecumseh.—Conduct of Hull.—Expedition to the River Raisin.—Capture of Chicago.—Battle of the River Raisin.—General Harrison's Campaign.—Commodore Perry.—His Victory on Lake Erie.—General Harrison arrives at Malden.—Marches to Detroit.—Battle of the Thames.—Death of Tecumseh.—His Character.—Attack on Mackinaw.—Peace Concluded.

In June, 1812, war was declared between Great Britain and the United States. Without entering into particulars as to the causes of this war, suffice it to say that it was chiefly provoked by the continued impressment of American seamen, the unjust capture of American vessels, and the enforcement of illegal blockades.

Governor Hull, the year before, had represented to the general government the exposed and defenceless condition of Michigan. That the posts at Detroit, Mackinaw, and Chicago were badly fortified and with insufficient garrisons, while at no great distance from them there was a large body of British subjects, who could, in case of war, be brought against them; that the whole American force consisted of but about five thousand men, whereas the militia of Canada amounted to more than one hundred thousand; and that the forests about Detroit were filled with hostile savages, who were secretly pledged to the confederacy of Tecumseh. This post he represented as of great importance, inasmuch as it commanded a wide extent of country, and furnished a point of support for operations against the Indians of the upper lakes. He proposed, therefore, that a powerful naval armament should be equipped on Lake Erie, sufficient to command that inland sea, and to co-operate effectively with the force at Detroit; or, if that were not done, that a strong detachment of troops should be marched from Niagara, to act in conjunction with those under his command in the invasion of the British provinces.*

A body of troops was soon collected at Dayton, in Ohio, consisting of about twelve hundred men, raised by order of the President of the United States, and their number was somewhat increased by volunteers. These troops were formed into three regiments, under the command of Colonels M'Arthur, Finelly, and Cass, and a fourth regiment, about three hundred strong, under Col. Miller, afterward joined them, the whole being under

* American State Papers.

the command of General Hull, the governor of Michigan.

With this force General Hull marched from Dayton towards Detroit, and soon arrived at the Maumee of the lakes. The dense forests through which they had to pass, wholly without roads, opposed formidable obstacles to their progress. At the rapids of the Maumee a vessel was procured for the transportation of the sick soldiers, and of such bulky articles as would encumber the army. As this vessel was proceeding for Detroit by the way of the channel leading to Malden, she was captured by the British, who communicated to the Americans the first news of the declaration of war.*

On the fifth of July General Hull arrived at Detroit, where his troops immediately set themselves to work to prepare for the coming contest. Four days afterward he received a communication from the secretary of war, investing him with discretionary power either to seize Malden and advance into Canada, or to remain on the defensive. That place formed the most prominent and commanding position upon this part of the lake coast, and its possession would give him advantages in any future operations against the provinces of Canada.

He therefore crossed the Detroit River with his

* Willard.

army, and established himself at Sandwich. From his headquarters at this place he issued a proclamation* addressed to the Canadians, setting forth his objects in invading their country, and inviting them to place themselves under the protection of the United States; protesting, at the same time, against the barbarity of employing the savages, and threatening indiscriminate retaliation against all who should be found fighting by their side.† It was hoped that by this means the French Canadians would be induced either to join the Americans or remain neutral.

Many of the American officers were anxious to proceed immediately to the attack of Malden, but it was determined to wait for heavy artillery to be brought from Detroit. The army therefore remained quietly at Sandwich, merely sending out occasional foraging parties to procure provisions.

General Hull wished to ascertain what was the actual state of things at Malden, and he accordingly detached Colonel Cass, with two hundred and eighty men, to reconnoitre that position. On reaching the River Canard, he dislodged a picket-guard of the enemy, killing ten of their number,

* This energetic and well-written address is said to have been from the pen of Governor, then Colonel, Cass.—*See Appendix* F.

† Brannan's Official Letters.

and seizing the bridge which they had been stationed there to defend. This bridge was only about four miles from Malden, and Colonel Cass was anxious to keep possession of it, to aid them in their contemplated attack upon that place. This, however, was thought inexpedient by General Hull, as such a course, he said, would bring on a general engagement, which he wished at that moment to avoid, as his artillery had not yet arrived, and a considerable detachment had been sent away from his army.*

While the Americans were thus stationary at Sandwich, a British force was despatched from the Canada side to take possession of the island of Mackinaw. The whole garrison of this post was only fifty-seven men, under the command of Lieutenant Hanks; and the first intimation which this officer received of the declaration of war was the arrival of a body of British troops, supported by more than a thousand Indian warriors, consisting of Sioux, Winnebagoes, Talleswain Ottawas, and Chippewas. The savages, it appears, had been directed, in case of resistance, to show no quarter, and the odds being so fearfully against him, the American officer immediately surrendered. A detachment, under the command of Capt. Brush, had been sent by Governor Meigs, of Ohio, to escort

* Whiting's Discourse.

a quantity of provisions destined for the American army, and General Hull, being informed that a body of Indians had left Malden to intercept this convoy, despatched Major Van Horn, with two hundred men, for its protection. On arriving at Brownstown, this detachment was suddenly attacked by the savages, who, from behind a breastwork of logs and the trunks of trees, opened a deadly fire upon the American troops. Major Van Horn, finding himself unable to contend against the superior numbers of the enemy, retreated to Detroit, leaving eighteen of his men dead on the field.*

The ordnance he was waiting for from Detroit not having arrived, on the 8th of August General Hull convened a council of war for the purpose of deciding what should be done, when it was determined to remain two days longer, and at the expiration of that time to make an attempt upon Malden at all hazards. Information, however, having been received in the mean time that the garrison at Malden had been re-enforced, General Hull changed his resolution, withdrew his army from the British territory, and retired to Detroit. The reasons he assigned for so unexpected a movement were, that General Brock was on his way to Malden with a considerable body of fresh troops; that his commu-

* Whiting's Discourse.

nication with Detroit was in danger of being cut off; and that the savage bands from the upper lakes, having no farther occupation in that quarter, would soon be pouring down upon him.

As it was important to open a communication with the River Raisin, that the army might receive the supplies sent from Ohio, six hundred men, under Lieutenant-colonel Miller, had been detached by General Hull for that object the day that he crossed the Detroit River to Frenchtown. Scarcely had this body reached Monguagon, when they were attacked by a superior force of British and Indians, the latter led on by Tecumseh, who opened upon them a destructive fire from their usual lurking-places behind trees and fallen timber, and in thickets of brushwood. The enemy being protected by a dense forest on the left, Colonel Miller advanced into it with his whole line, ordering his men to deliver a single fire, and then charge with the bayonet. This was gallantly done, and the British, as well as their savage allies, gave way before the fury of the onset. But, though thrown into confusion and broken, they still continued to fight with the utmost desperation. Tecumseh, although wounded, was seen in the thickest of the battle, and his shrill war-cry was heard above the fire of the musketry. An Indian, whose leg had been broken by a musket-ball, while writhing with the agony of his wound, loaded his rifle and shot an American horseman. Many of the savages had stationed themselves in the tops of the trees, from which they discharged their rifles and arrows with deadly aim. The British force was commanded by Major Muir, of the forty-first regiment, and was four hundred strong without the Indians. The American loss in the action was ten non-commissioned officers and privates killed and forty-five wounded of the regular troops, and eight killed and forty-five wounded of the Ohio and Michigan volunteers. The British retreated under the cover of their armed vessels, which were anchored in the Detroit River, while the savages scattered themselves in the woods.

It was now determined to bring in the supplies needed for the army by a more circuitous route, and Colonels M'Arthur and Cass, with three hundred and fifty of the best troops, were detached from Detroit on the 13th of August for that object.

On the 14th the British General Brock arrived at Malden, and, advancing immediately to Sandwich with all his forces, the following day he summoned General Hull to surrender. "It is far from my intention," he said, "to join in a war of extermination, but you must be aware that the numerous body of Indians who have attached themselves to my troops will be beyond my control the moment the contest commences." To this menace the American general answered, "I have no other reply to make than that I am prepared to meet any force which may be at your disposal."

The character of General Hull seems to have been well understood by the British commander. Indeed, in addition to the evidence he had given of indecision in not advancing against Malden, it was alleged that a portion of his correspondence, found on board an American vessel captured near that place, but too clearly evinced a want of those qualities which should distinguish a military commander.*

Tecumseh, with his warriors, was at this time with the British general, to aid him in his projected attack upon the American post; and the latter, being anxious to acquire some knowledge of the country around Detroit, that he might avail himself of it in case he should from any cause be obliged to retreat into the neighbouring forest, applied to this chief for information. Tecumseh took a strip of elm bark, stretched it upon the ground, and placed a stone upon each corner. Then with his scalping knife he delineated upon it an accurate representation of the country, with its swamps, woods, and rivers. Pleased with this display of ingenuity, and to show his gratitude for the impor-

* Whiting's Discourse.

tant services which this renowned chief had rendered to the British cause, Brock took his sash from his waist and presented it to him. The savage, however, would not wear it, but gave it to the Wyandot chief Round-Head, "because," said he, "he is an older and better warrior than I am." Before the British crossed to the American side, their commander expressed a hope that the Indians, in case Detroit was taken, would not massacre the defenceless inhabitants. "No," answered Tecumseh; "I despise them too much to have anything to do with them."

As soon as he received the refusal to capitulate, Brock commenced a cannonade upon the American fort from across the river. This was answered from the opposite shore with considerable effect. An armed vessel being now seen about a mile below Detroit, it was supposed that the British intended to cross there, and Captain Snelling was detached with a body of troops to prevent it. It was suggested at the same time that a single piece of heavy ordnance would compel the British armed vessel to remove from her position, and keep the enemy from landing. This advice was, however, disregarded, and Captain Snelling was recalled to the fort by break of day.*

Very early on the morning of the 16th, the whole

* Whiting's Discourse.

British force was seen slowly crossing the river, under cover of their armed vessel, and they soon landed, and advanced to Springwells without opposition. Here they halted, while the British general sent a second summons to the commander of the American post to surrender. It was not long, however, before the enemy was again seen advancing, his force being composed of regulars, and of volunteers dressed in British uniforms, approaching nearer and nearer, as they moved deliberately through the forest bordering on the river, supported by their Indian allies under Maissot, Walk-in-the-Water, and Tecumseh. The American soldiers were impatiently waiting for orders to fire upon the advancing column, when all at once a white flag was hoisted upon the walls of the fort. General Hull, with cannon planted, and poised to carry destruction into the ranks of the enemy, with a force which, to say the least, could have successfully resisted any immediate attack, suddenly gave orders that the detachments posted outside of the pickets and those on the ramparts should retire within the fort. Detroit, in a word, was given up without a shot being fired. The American soldiers dashed their muskets upon the ground in an agony of mingled shame and indignation. The regular troops were surrendered as prisoners of war, all the public property was given up, and no stipulations were made in behalf of the Canadian allies. The honour of the American arms was tarnished, and General Hull was disgraced forever. The detachments under Colonel Cass and Captain Brush had been included in the capitulation, but they fortunately escaped the disgrace that had been prepared for them.

General Hull was tried for treason and cowardice before a court-martial, and, though acquitted on the first charge, was convicted on the second, and sentenced to be shot; but, in consideration of his former services in the war of the Revolution, he was pardoned by the president.*

There would seem to be no doubt that the conduct of General Hull was not that of a brave and efficient officer. He neglected to advance into Canada when he might have done so with a fair prospect of success; he evinced a want of firmness in resisting the enemy; and, finally, he gave up an important post, that was prepared for a siege, without firing a gun in its defence; surrendering, at the same time, the entire territory under his charge.

On the other hand, it has been said in his defence that he was in the midst of an immense wilderness, filled with savages, where he was cut off from all aid from the East. It has been alleged,

* Whiting's Discourse.

too, that a spirit of insubordination prevailed among the militia, and that party strife among them ran high. But we would draw a veil over the subject. This much is in his favour, that the verdict of the court exonerated him from the guilt of treason, whatever might have been the verdict of his country.

Meantime, the military post of Chicago also capitulated. Influenced by a fear of the hostile Indians on the borders of Lake Michigan, General Hull had, on the first breaking out of the war, ordered Captain Heald, the commander of this post, to abandon it and retire to Fort Wayne. A large body of savages had collected around it, and they were promised all the surplus stores if they would abstain from harassing the detachment on its withdrawal from the fort. There was among these stores a quantity of powder and whiskey, either of which it was thought imprudent to relinquish to the Indians; the former was accordingly deposited in a well, and the latter thrown away. The savages, however, found out what had been done, and they were perceived collecting around the fort, apparently with hostile intentions. The garrison, consisting of fifty-four regulars and twelve militiamen, accompanied by twelve families who had fled there for protection, retired from the post, and had not proceeded more than half a mile when they were attacked by the savages. Having imprudently destroyed the means of defending themselves, they were soon compelled to surrender, which they did not do, however, until about half their number had been killed, and several of the women and children. The prisoners were distributed among the neighbouring tribes, and on the following morning the fort was set on fire and burned to the ground.

Being now in possession of Michigan, the British established a provisionary government at Detroit, the savages, meanwhile, being permitted at pleasure to ravage the frontier settlements and insult the defenceless inhabitants.

But, although the British arms had been thus far successful, it was determined to wrest from them the advantages they had gained. Accordingly, three separate armies were assembled: that of the North, stationed upon the shores of Lake Champlain, and under the command of General Hampton; that of the centre, between Lakes Ontario and Erie, under General Dearborn; and that of the West, under General Harrison, to take up its position at the head of Lake Erie. The protection of the Michigan frontier, therefore, devolved more immediately upon the latter.* The defence of Upper Canada was at this time committed to Colonels Proctor and Vincent, and that of the lower province to General Sheaffe, under the direction of the governor-general of the provinces.

* Whiting's Discourse.

General Harrison lost no time in marching his army towards the lake frontier. He sent forward a detachment of his forces to Presque Isle, to wait there for the arrival of the main body; and General Winchester, with eight hundred Kentuckians, was ordered to advance to Frenchtown, on the River Raisin, where he arrived on the 13th of January.

This officer took up a position on the Frenchtown side of the river, close to its banks. Sentinels were placed around the encampment, and the night being cold, the troops spent the greater part of it in ranging about the village. During the evening, a French Canadian from Malden gave information that a body of British and Indians, amounting in all to about three thousand men, were preparing to start from that place for the River Raisin soon after he left. No notice, however, was taken of this intelligence, from a belief that it was without any foundation, and, consequently, no precautionary measures were adopted, the main road by which alone the enemy could pass being left entirely unguarded. So completely unapprehensive, indeed, was the American commander of any danger, that he had taken lodgings on the opposite bank of the river, at the house of a Frenchman.

Early on the morning of the 22d of January, just after the *reveillé* had been beat, a rapid fire of musketry was heard from the sentinels. The enemy, it appears, had arrived without being observed during the night, and taken up a position behind a small ravine, from which he now opened a tremendous fire of shells, and of grape and cannon shot, upon the American camp. The consternation of the Americans was greatly increased by the advance of the British troops under Proctor, and by the fiendish yells of the savages. A general panic ensued, and great numbers were cut down. In the mean time, General Winchester arrived from the opposite shore, and attempted to rally his retreating soldiers; but, exposed as they were to a heavy fire from the enemy, they continued to fall back. Orders were then given to incline towards the centre, and retire within the pickets of their camp. These orders, however, appear not to have been heard, and the troops, pressed by the bayonets of the British regulars, and attacked by the savages on their right, retreated in great confusion upon the ice across the river.*

An attempt was now made to re-enforce the right wing, but without success. Owing to the suddenness of the attack, and the want of all preparation to meet it, there was neither system, discipline, nor obedience. The savages had posted themselves along the edge of the surrounding forest, at every

* Dawson.

point where there was any chance for retreat. They also completely commanded the long narrow lane leading to the village, and here great numbers of the Americans were killed. On the borders of the wood, the two chiefs Round-Head and Split-Log urged on their warriors to the commission of the most frightful cruelties, and here the tomahawk and scalping-knife were dyed in blood. Colonel Allen was shot down, but Majors Graves and Madison continued gallantly to maintain their position within the pickets against all the attacks of the British, supported by their savage allies. General Winchester had in the mean time been taken prisoner; and not long after, a flag arrived from the British lines with orders addressed to Major Madison from that officer to cease hostilities, and surrender his troops prisoners of war. To this the former replied, that as the Indians were in the habit of massacring their prisoners, he would agree to no capitulation unless the safety of his men was first expressly guarantied. The surrender was finally adjusted upon the conditions that the lives of the soldiers should be protected, that individual property should be held sacred, that sleds should be sent the next morning with the wounded to Amherstburgh, and that the sidearms of the officers should be restored at Malden. The battle-field was covered with the lifeless forms of the brave

Kentuckians, who but a few hours before were seen full of hope, and glowing with all the ardour of patriotism. The painted savage and the British regular, the ardent and chivalrous son of high promise, who had been nursed in the lap of luxury, and the hardy yeoman, with his sleeves bared for battle, as they had been before rolled up while guiding the plough across his peaceful prairies, lay side by side on this field of death.*

Shortly after the action, Colonel Proctor marched away with his regular troops and most of his savage allies, the remainder being left to guard the prisoners. At about sunrise the next morning, however, most of the Indians were seen coming back, painted in the most hideous manner, and in a state of intoxication. It was not long before they set up their horrid yells, and, rushing into the houses where the wounded prisoners were lying, they tore from them their blankets, and then despatched them with their tomahawks. Among these unhappy men there was a young Kentuckian of extraordinary beauty. Struck with his perfect proportions and manly grace, a chief claimed him as his prize, and led him in triumph, and in seeming admiration, through the village. But this was only in mockery of his victim; the tomahawk was commissioned to do its horrid work, and his cluster-

* Dawson.

ing ringlets were soon seen waving from the scalp-stick of the merciless savage.

Most of the prisoners were confined in two houses. These the savages set on fire, and, as their victims attempted to escape from the windows, they pushed them back into the flames. Major Woolfolk, General Winchester's secretary, was shot dead in the street; and, to complete the atrocity of this bloody transaction, the bodies of those who were slain were left where they fell, to feed the wolves of the neighbouring forest. The condition of such of the prisoners as escaped immediate death was not much better. These were marched towards Malden; and as soon as, from fatigue and exhaustion, they were unable to proceed farther, they were immediately despatched, and their bodies left unburied.

Meantime General Harrison was in Ohio, making every effort in his power to overcome the difficulties by which he was surrounded. Michigan, from the nature and position of the country, separated as it was by a dense forest from the inhabited portions of the United States, and occupied by savage tribes hostile to their cause, was a conquest of great value to the British. It gave them the command, too, of the posts on the upper lakes, and thus they were enabled to control the resources of the vast tract of territory along those inland seas, and of the country extending from the western borders of Indiana and Illinois to the mouth of the Maumee.

Thus completely in the possession of the British and Indians, and protected by the intervening forests, Lake Erie seemed to be the only channel by which Michigan could be approached with a prospect of recovering it from the enemy. It became, therefore, an object of great importance to obtain the mastery on that lake, which was then commanded by an English fleet under Commodore Barclay.

At this conjuncture, Oliver Hazard Perry, a young officer twenty-eight years of age, then in charge of a flotilla of gun-boats at Newport, anxious to obtain more active service, turned his attention to this lake; and his views having been approved of by the naval department, he proceeded without loss of time to the port of Erie, for the purpose of building and equipping a fleet there, sufficiently powerful to give him the command of its waters.* A braver or more efficient officer could have been nowhere found. He was in the prime of early manhood, active, vigorous, and intelligent, generous and self-sacrificing even to a fault, and possessed of those fine moral traits which gave a finish to his character, and admirably har-

* Cooper.

monized with the manly beauty of his person. He laboured with indefatigable zeal to hasten the construction and equipment of his vessels, and, after encountering and overcoming every kind of discouragement, he at length found himself in the command of a sufficient force to meet the enemy. As, however, there was a difficulty in crossing the bar at the mouth of the harbour, and he was closely watched by the British commander, he remained quietly at anchor in port until a favourable opportunity should occur to sally forth. At length the fortunate moment arrived, and the American fleet was got safely over the bar, and made its way towards the upper end of the lake. On reaching Put-in Bay, Captain Perry there came to anchor, impatient for an opportunity to measure his strength with the enemy, and to wrest from him the superiority on this inland sea.

On the 10th of September, at dawn of day, as their anchors were apeak, and the crews of the different vessels were shaking out their topgallant-sails, the enemy were seen bearing down, under light sail, in order of battle, with their hulls newly painted, and the crimson flag of England waving at their mastheads. The British fleet, consisting of the ships Detroit, carrying nineteen guns, the Queen Charlotte, of seventeen guns, the schooner Lady Prevost, of thirteen guns, the brig Hunter, of ten guns, the sloop Little Belt, of three guns, and the schooner Chippewa, of one gun and mounting two swivels, was commanded by a veteran officer of tried skill and valour.

The British vessels no sooner made their appearance than the American fleet prepared for action and stood out upon the lake. It consisted of the brigs Lawrence, of twenty guns; Niagara, of twenty guns; Caledonia, of three guns; the schooners Ariel, of four guns; Scorpion, of two guns; Somers, of two guns; the sloop Trippe, of one gun; and the schooners Tigress and Porcupine, each of one gun.*

While the two fleets were thus approaching each other, the savages were not idle. Tecumseh had stationed himself with a band of warriors upon the island at the mouth of the Detroit River, waiting with intense interest the issue of the contest. No sooner was any change made in the movements of the hostile squadrons, than he paddled swiftly over to Malden to communicate the fact. From the first roar of their guns he predicted the success of the English, and was greatly surprised when the news was brought to him that they had struck their colours to the Americans.

The order of battle decided on by Commodore Perry was to attack the Detroit, the British flag-

* Cooper.

ship, himself with the Lawrence, to oppose the Niagara to the Royal Charlotte, and the rest of his fleet was ordered to act as circumstances might require, and assail the enemy as they should be directed by signals, while the Ariel and Scorpion were instructed to take a position on the weather-bow and ahead of the Lawrence, in order to draw off a portion of the fire from that ship.

As the two fleets neared each other, the action was commenced by the enemy's flag-ship, the Detroit, she being mounted with long guns, while the American vessels had only short pieces. The American commander, resolved to capture the hostile fleet or perish in the attempt, bore down directly for the Detroit, making signals at the same time for all his vessels to come into close action. Owing to causes which are not very clearly understood, the Niagara did not bear down to his aid. Still he was undaunted, although alone, and exposed to nearly the whole of the enemy's fire. Ranging along the front of their squadron, single and unsupported, he successively poured upon their ships from the battery of the Lawrence tremendous broadsides of ball and grape, while he received from them, in return, a no less destructive fire, which shivered his spars, and covered his decks with wounded and dead. Such a fire no single vessel could long withstand. The hull of his ship was pierced in every direction, twenty-one of his men had been killed, sixty-one were wounded, and only fifteen remained who were capable of duty. All of his cannon except one had been dismounted, and this he continued to work with his own hands.*

His ship being thus a complete wreck, and incapable of being longer defended, he determined to abandon her; and ordering his boat, amid a shower of shot he proceeded to the Niagara, which vessel then lay at a considerable distance, and had not been yet brought into close action. Meeting Captain Elliott at the gangway, he requested him to take the boat in which he had come and bring up the rest of the vessels, while he himself would bear down upon the enemy with the Niagara. The flag of the Lawrence now came down, amid the cheers of the British sailors, who supposed that the American fleet had struck. Ordering every sail on board the Niagara to be set, he was not long in closing with the enemy's ships; and passing along their line, he poured upon them, in quick succession, tremendous broadsides. Having driven the Royal Charlotte out of line, he next attacked the Detroit, and by the severity of his fire drove her men from their quarters. Captain Elliott now came up with the smaller vessels, and, taking a raking position

* Slidell's Naval Sketches.

under the stern of the Detroit, assisted to complete the victory. The slaughter on board this ship was dreadful: twenty-seven of her men had been killed and ninety-six wounded. At length a white handkerchief was hung out on the end of a boarding-pike as a signal of surrender; the triumph was complete, and all the vessels of the enemy were taken. The dead of both fleets were buried on an island in the lake.

The conduct of Perry was no less distinguished by humanity after the action than it had been by skill and bravery while the battle was raging; and the British commander long afterward expressed his grateful recollection of the generous courtesy of his youthful conqueror. It is thus that the horrors of war are in some degree softened by a display of the kindlier feelings of our nature.*

This brilliant success gave to the Americans the uncontrolled command of the lake, and on the 23d of September their fleet landed twelve hundred men near Malden. Colonel Proctor, however, had previously evacuated that post, after setting fire to the fort and to the public storehouses. Commodore Perry in the mean time passed up to Detroit with the Ariel, to assist in the occupation of that town, while Captain Elliott, with the Lady Prevost,

* See Mackenzie's Life of Perry, vol. ii.

the Scorpion, and the Tigress, advanced into Lake St. Clair to intercept the enemy's stores.*

Thus General Harrison, on his arrival at Detroit and Malden, found both places abandoned by the enemy, and was met by the Canadians asking for his protection. Tecumseh proposed to the British commander that they should hazard an engagement at Malden ; but the latter foresaw that he should be exposed to the fire of the American fleet in that position, and therefore resolved to march to the Moravian towns upon the Thames, near St. Clair Lake, above Detroit, and there try the chance of a battle.

His force at this time consisted of about nine hundred regular troops, and fifteen hundred Indians commanded by Tecumseh. The American army amounted to two thousand seven hundred men, of whom one hundred and twenty were regulars, a considerable number militia, about thirty Indians, and the remainder Kentucky riflemen, well mounted, and mainly young men, full of ardour, and burning with a desire to revenge the massacre of their friends and relatives at the River Raisin.

The American general lost no time in seeking the enemy, whom he found drawn up in order of battle, and prepared to receive him. On his right, in a swamp, was posted Tecumseh with his Indian

* Cooper.

warriors, while the space between them and the river was occupied by the regular troops. The American general extended his line to the same length with that of the British infantry, his small body of regulars he ordered to seize the enemy's artillery, and the few friendly Indians were directed to act on his flank.*

It had been determined to penetrate the swamp and turn the right of the Indians, as they could not cross the river, and the infantry were on the point of making this movement, when it was ascertained that the British were drawn up in a double line, and that, to enable them to occupy the whole space between the swamp and the river, they had been obliged to open their files. The plan of attack was therefore changed, and Colonel Johnson, with his mounted Kentuckians, was ordered to charge the enemy in front. These brave volunteers rushed upon the British column with such impetuosity that, unable to resist the fierceness of the onset, it broke and fled. Cleared of the regular force of the enemy, the battle-field now exhibited a series of personal encounters between the Kentuckians and Indians. Tecumseh, being wounded, it is said, and exasperated to desperation by the flight of his allies, resolved to sell his life as dearly as possible. Rushing, therefore, into the

* Willard.

hottest of the conflict, he soon fell, pierced by a pistol-ball, and instantly expired.

This renowned chief deserves a passing notice. He possessed a noble figure, his countenance was strikingly expressive of magnanimity, and he was distinguished by moral traits far above his race. He was not remarkable for eloquence or even for intellect, but he was a warrior in the broadest Indian sense of the word. Without the far-reaching views of Pontiac or his hereditary rank, still, in sudden action and desperate valour, he showed himself superior to that chief; and, though a new man, he acquired unbounded influence, and placed himself above all competitors as the great champion of Indian rights. While his brother, the Prophet, was the principal manager of the confederacy in all that related to its organization and plans, he was its executive arm in the field. There were other peculiarities by which he was no less distinguished. Like Pontiac, he manifested a deep interest in regard to the manners and customs of the whites; he would not sanction the barbarities practised by the Indians, and he disdained the personal adornments in which they so much delight. Although holding the rank of a brigadier-general in the British service, he pertinaciously adhered to his Indian garb; a deerskin coat, with leggins of the same material, was his constant dress, and in his he was found dead at the battle of the Thames. During the latter years of his life he was almost incessantly engaged either in the council or at the head of his warlike bands, and he sunk at last on the field of his glory, with tomahawk in hand and the cry of battle upon his lips.

> " Like monumental bronze, unchanged his look,
> A soul which pity touch'd, but never shook ;
> Train'd, from his tree-rock'd cradle to his bier,
> The fierce extremes of good and ill to brook ;
> Unchanging, fearing but the shame of fear,
> A stoic of the woods, a man without a tear."

With the death of Tecumseh the confederacy was dissolved, and a peace was concluded with the Ottawas, Chippewas, Miamis, and Pottawatamies.

The American fleet was now employed in removing the ammunition and stores from the captured British posts; and on the 18th of October General Harrison and Commodore Perry issued a joint proclamation at Detroit for the better government of the territory of Michigan, and guarantying to the inhabitants their rights of property, and the enjoyment of their ancient usages and laws.

The island of Mackinaw was now the only part of the territory remaining in the possession of the enemy. This being a post of great importance, from its commanding the upper lakes, and being the centre of the fur-trade, a fleet under Commodore Sinclair, with a body of land forces under

Colonel Croghan, the gallant defender of Sandusky, was despatched in July, 1814, for the purpose of capturing it. After reconnoitring the coast near the island, the commodore proceeded to the neighbouring island of St. Joseph, where he destroyed a few trading-posts and then returned.

Meanwhile, the British commandant was actively employed in strengthening his defences, and in summoning to his aid the nearest savage tribes. It was at first proposed to attack the post near the village, as that part was the most free from trees, and, consequently, afforded less covert to the Indians. This, however, was objected to by Sinclair, as his fleet would be here exposed to the fire of the fort. It was finally concluded to land on the north-eastern side of the island, although from this point they would be obliged to traverse its whole breadth, through a dense forest, in order to reach the British position. After marching some distance through the wilderness, on arriving at a small clearing, the detachment was fired on from all sides by the savages stationed in the surrounding woods. Major Holmes, at the head of a considerable force, was directed to charge the enemy; but, as he was gallantly executing the order, he was shot down by a rifle-ball. The fire, indeed, was so destructive, that the advanced party was obliged to retreat to the main body, upon which the whole force retired to their boats, abandoned the enterprise, and returned to Detroit. In consequence of this failure, the British retained possession of Mackinaw until the conclusion of peace.

The victory of Commodore Perry having secured the command of Lake Erie, Proctor's army having been routed and the Indian confederacy broken up, nothing of special interest transpired in Michigan during the remainder of the war. Colonel Cass was left with a brigade for the protection of the territory, which he effectually accomplished, until the treaty of peace, concluded at Ghent on the 17th of February, 1815, put an end to all farther hostilities.

CHAPTER X.

Lewis Cass appointed Governor of the Territory.—Its Condition at that Time.—Public Lands brought into Market.—First Steamboat on the Lakes.—University Founded.—Expedition to Explore the Lakes.—The Clinton Canal.—Mr. Porter appointed Governor.—Mode of making Surveys.—Controversy with Ohio.—Mr. Mason elected Governor.—State Organized.—Internal Improvements.—Education.—Conclusion.

MICHIGAN now emerged into a new existence. Colonel Cass, who had served with great credit during the war, was appointed governor of the territory, and under his administration it gradually advanced in prosperity.

Hitherto there had been but little inducement for immigration from the East: the public lands had not been brought into the market, and recently the country had been suffering under the devastation of war. The beautiful oak-openings on the Kalamazoo, the fertile tracts on the borders of Grand River, the prairies of the St. Joseph, and the rich and inviting slopes along the shores of Lake Michigan, were traversed only by the wild beast and the savage, and the streams navigated only by the bark canoe. The feeble settlements on the frontier had been converted into scenes of desolation; no roads through the interior had been constructed; and the only access to the country by land from the East was through the trackless wilderness distinguished by the name of the Black Swamp, and by the military road along the Detroit River. Everything, therefore, was to be done to develop the resources of the territory, and to secure to it the advantages which, from its position and the fertility of its soil, it was entitled to enjoy.

It would appear, however, that the character of the country in regard to the latter particular was at that time but little understood, as is shown by the following fact. In 1812, Congress had passed an act providing for the survey of the bounty-lands to be granted to the soldiers enlisting for the war which had then just commenced, and this survey was directed to be made in the territory of Michi gan. The persons employed for this object, however, made so unfavourable a report in regard to the soil, representing it as marshy and everywhere steril, that in 1816 the act was repealed, and the quantity of land required for this purpose was ordered to be surveyed in Arkansas and Illinois. The surveyors either did not make a thorough examination of the soil, or, what perhaps is more probable, they were deceived by the sandy nature of the oak-lands, which have a yellowish colour before they are brought into cultivation, but which, from the quantity of lime they contain, turn black after they are exposed to the action of the sun and air by the plough.

During that year, however, and the two following, the country was more fully explored, and numerous tracts of fertile land, with a rolling surface, variegated by groves and lakes, were discovered. These lands were forthwith surveyed, and in 1817 and 1818 portions of them were offered for sale,* showing the superiority of our enlightened and liberal laws, contrasted with the narrow policy of the former possessors of the soil. A great change now took place in public opinion in regard to the value of these lands, and subsequent surveys more fully confirmed the inaccuracy of the impressions which had hitherto prevailed in relation to them.

With the introduction of steam navigation upon its vast inland seas, a new era may be said to have commenced in the history of the progress of the West. This was in 1819, when the first steamboat, the Walk-in-the-Water, made her appearance on Lake Erie, crossing that lake and passing up to Mackinaw.†

By the census taken about that time, the population of Michigan was ascertained to be eight thousand eight hundred and ninety-six. Detroit contained two hundred and fifty houses, and fourteen

* Biddle's Discourse. † Schoolcraft.

hundred and fifteen inhabitants, independent of the garrison. The island of Mackinaw, which continued to be a central mart for the fur-trade, had a stationary population of four hundred and fifty, which was at times increased to not less than two thousand by the Indians and traders who resorted there from the upper lakes. The settlement at the Sault de Ste. Marie contained only fifteen or twenty houses, occupied by French and English families.

Although, by the ordinance of 1787, lot number 16 was directed to be reserved in every township for the support of common schools, no measures had yet been taken to introduce a system of public instruction, if we except the act passed by the governor and judges in 1817 for the establishment of what was styled in it the *Catholepestemiad,* or University of Michigan. This act, which was drawn up by Augustus B. Woodward, chief justice of the territory, is a very curious document. He was a gentleman possessing extensive acquirements, but was not a little eccentric in his character, and the views he entertained on this and some other subjects were certainly not very practical. The phraseology of the act is not its least singular feature, and would seem better suited to the age of my Lord Coke than to the understanding and condition of a race of new settlers engaged in clearing away the forest. This University was to have thirteen *didaxia* or professorships,* each of which was to be liberally endowed, and it was designed to lay broad and deep the foundations for a thorough education.

Indeed, all Judge Woodward's projects seem to have been upon no very moderate scale. Detroit is indebted to him for a plan of the city laid out in the form of a *cobweb*, with public squares, a circus, a *Campus Martius*, streets, cross-streets, avenues, &c., more vast in its conception and more complex in its design than ancient Rome, and requiring a longer period to fill it up than from the time of Romulus to our own day. The utilitarian tendencies of his successors, however, have made strange havoc with this magnificent plan, the traces of which are now nowhere visible but on the map.

On the admission of Illinois into the Union in 1818, all the territory lying north of that state and Indiana was annexed to Michigan; and the following year Congress passed an act authorizing the election of a delegate from the territory to the national Legislature, who should have the right of speaking, but not of voting. This was of great advantage to the inhabitants, as they were thereby provided with a representative through whom they

* See Territorial Act of 1817.

could make known their wants to the general government.

Michigan, meanwhile, gradually continued to advance in population. The settlers extended themselves along the banks of the Rivers Raisin, Huron, and St. Clair, and cleared away the forest from the spots where now stand the villages of Ann Arbor, Ypsilanti, Pontiac, Jackson, and Tecumseh.

That portion of the territory, however, situated upon the borders of the upper lakes, was then but little known; and in 1820 an expedition was set on foot for the purpose of exploring it, to ascertain the numbers and condition of the Indian tribes in that quarter, and to select such positions as might be most favourable for its defence. This expedition, which was under the direction of Governor Cass, was accompanied by a mineralogist, a topographical engineer, and a physician; was provided with an escort of soldiers, and the commanding officers of the posts along the lakes were ordered to afford to it every facility in their power. The party started from Detroit on the 24th of May, in bark canoes, manned by *voyageurs* and Indians.

Passing up the River St. Clair, they proceeded along the shores of Lake Huron, visited the island of Mackinaw, then maintained as a trading-post by the Northwest Company, and soon arrived at the Sault de Ste. Marie.*

This was considered a favourable point for the establishment of a military post. By the treaty of Greenville, concluded in 1795, the Indians had agreed that all the lands which they had granted to the French or English should be transferred to the United States. This place they had ceded to the French, who formerly maintained a garrison here: it was clear, therefore, that it came within the provisions of that treaty. A council was therefore called, at which the Indian chiefs attended, dressed in fine broadcloths and decorated with trinkets of British manufacture. The savages opposed the proposed occupation, and sought to prevent it by denying all knowledge of the original cession; and when it was fully explained to them, they still persisted in withholding their consent, though in less positive terms, suggesting that their young men might prove unruly, and kill the cattle which should stray from the post. This being understood as intended for a threat, Governor Cass replied that he would give himself no farther trouble to confer on the subject, but that, as sure as the rising sun would set in the west, so sure should an American garrison be established at that place, whatever might be their decision.†

* Schoolcraft's Journal. † Ibid.

The chiefs, who appear to have been under British influence, now spent several hours in discussion. Some of them were willing that the Americans should occupy the post if there were no troops stationed there. At length a chief, who held the rank of a brigadier-general in the British service, seized his war-lance and struck it furiously on the ground, intimating thereby that the place would not be given up except to superior force, and the council soon afterward dispersed in a hostile spirit.

The expedition under Governor Cass consisted of sixty-six men, of whom thirty were regular soldiers, and the savages numbered about eighty warriors. The latter occupied the site of the old French fort, and the Americans were drawn up upon the bank of the River St. Mary, a ravine separating the two at a distance of five or six hundred yards.*

While the Americans were waiting to see what would be the issue of the affair, the British flag was hoisted from the midst of the Indian encampment by the chief who had shown so hostile a disposition in the council. On discovering this, Governor Cass ordered his men to stand by their arms, and, taking an interpreter, proceeded directly to the Indian camp. Here he indignantly tore down

* Schoolcraft's Journal.

the obnoxious flag, telling the chief who had hoisted it that it was an insult of the grossest kind; that the flag was the emblem of national sovereignty; that the ensigns of two different nations could never float on the same soil; that they would not be permitted to raise any other than that of the United States; and that, if they attempted it again, that power would set a strong foot upon their necks, and crush them to the earth. When he had said this the governor returned to his encampment, and a few minutes after he arrived there, the Indian women and children were seen quitting their lodges and getting on board their canoes. No act of hostility, however, was committed; and some of the older chiefs, who had not been present at the council, came forward and made overtures of peace. At seven o'clock the same evening a treaty was concluded with them, by which they ceded to the United States a tract of four miles square around the Sault, including the portage, the site of the old French fort, and the village, reserving to themselves the right of fishing at the falls, and of encamping upon the shores. The calumet was smoked, and blankets, knives, silver trinkets, and broadcloths were distributed among them.*

Everything having been settled, the expedition started again, and proceeded along the shores of

* Schoolcraft's Journal.

Lake Superior. Here they were struck with the appearance of the Pictured Rocks, which extend for miles along the shores of the lake, stained with a variety of hues by the washing of mineral waters, and which exhibit to the delighted beholder the most singular scene imaginable of Nature's painting. They visited also the Doric Rock, which presents the aspect of a rude though magnificent piece of architecture, chiselled from the solid granite, and examined other curiosities on this part of the coast. The Copper Rock, at the mouth of the Ontonagon River, which has from time immemorial been the subject of Indian superstition in this wild, sequestered region, they found particularly worthy of notice.

Having completed its survey, the expedition returned to Detroit by the way of Lake Michigan. The results were a more accurate knowledge of the geography of the country and of the operations of the Northwest Fur Company, the selection of sites for a line of military posts, and several important treaties with the Indian tribes, ceding valuable tracts of land to the United States. Mr. Henry R. Schoolcraft, who accompanied the expedition, afterward published his journal, giving a particular account of the country, and of the incidents which occurred along their route.

Soon after this an important change took place

in the government of the territory. In 1823 Congress passed an act abrogating the legislative power of the governor and judges, and establishing a legislative council, to consist of nine members, limiting also the judges' term of office to four years. Two years afterward all county officers, excepting those of a judicial character, were made elective by the people ; all executive appointments were required to be approved by the legislative council ; and an act was passed empowering the governor and council to divide the territory into townships, to incorporate the same, and to define their rights and privileges.*

The Erie Canal, which had been commenced in 1817, was in 1825 opened for navigation from the Hudson to Buffalo; and this event forms an important epoch in the progress of Michigan. The effect of this great public improvement on the interests of the West was twofold; it cheapened the foreign merchandise of which it stood in need, and in the same or a still greater proportion enhanced the price of its agricultural products. Its lands therefore increased in value, new facilities and new motives were offered for settlement, and from this period those vast and fertile regions advanced rapidly in population and general prosperity.

To meet the claims of the increasing population

* Territorial Laws.

of the territory, new privileges were granted. In 1827 the legislative council was made elective by the people, with the power of enacting laws, subject to the approval of Congress and the veto of the local executive ; and upon this footing things remained until the territory was admitted into the Union.

Governor Cass, meanwhile, was indefatigable in his efforts to have roads constructed through the interior, and, warned by the experience of the past, to provide effectually for the public defence. His whole administration, indeed, was characterized by a persevering zeal to promote the prosperity of Michigan ; to improve its institutions, and to develop its resources.

A new impulse, as we have already remarked, had been given to the progress of the West. It offered a boundless field for enterprise, and began to be considered the proper asylum and retreat for all who would better their fortune by industry. It was emphatically "the poor man's country," where his labour was sure to be rewarded by competence, and eventually by wealth. Hence population flowed in rapidly from the East. The hardy settlers, scattering over the country, made the woods resound with the stroke of the axe ; and everywhere the smoke of their cabins was seen

* Territorial Laws.

ascending from the depths of the forest. The lakes presented a no less animated scene: the white wings of commerce were spread out upon their waters, and the cloud from the distant steamer was seen stretching along the horizon. The reign of Nature in these hitherto silent and secluded solitudes was at an end, and that of man, with all its life, and bustle, and activity, had begun.

In 1831, General Cass, having been appointed secretary of war, was succeeded by Mr. George B. Porter in the government of the territory, the population of which at this time amounted to about thirty-five thousand. During his administration, Wisconsin, which had before been annexed to Michigan, was erected into a separate territory. Meantime the commerce on Lake Erie was rapidly increasing. A road, which was, to say the least, passable at some seasons of the year, was constructed across the Black Swamp, and numerous avenues were opened into the interior. In consequence of these improvements, the country became better known, a spirit of speculation was awakened, and, in addition to the actual settlers, the woods were traversed by numbers in search of desirable tracts, which they purchased at the government price, in the expectation of realizing large profits from their rapid increase in value.

The method adopted by the government in making their surveys is one of great accuracy. Two straight lines were drawn across the territory, the one running north and south, the other east and west. The north and south line was denominated the principal meridian, and the east and west line was called the base line. The territory was then divided into townships six miles square, and these were subdivided into thirty-six sections of a square mile each, the townships being numbered in regular order, commencing at the meridian and base lines, and increasing as they receded from them. The mathematical accuracy of this method, and the farther circumstance that each section and township, and also the lines of the sections, were blazed or marked upon the trees, enabled the emigrant, even in the depths of the forest, to find clear landmarks to guide his course, and to ascertain the actual boundaries of each tract. The smallest lot which can be purchased is one of eighty acres, or a fractional lot made by a township line or by the course of a stream.

Prior to the year 1820, the established government price for land was two dollars an acre, one fourth of which was required to be paid at the time of purchase, and the remainder in three annual instalments, the land being subject to forfeiture if these were not punctually paid, while a discount of eight per cent. was allowed if the whole amount was paid in advance. This system, how ever, was found to be productive of serious evils. The expectation of gain induced many to make large purchases, and while some realized fortunes, perhaps, from their investments, others, who were less successful, were without the means of paying their instalments, and thus the whole became liable to forfeiture. These results led to a total change of the system. The price of the public lands was reduced from two dollars to one dollar and a quarter the acre, the whole of which was required to be paid down at the time the purchase was made. This was attended with the best effects, preventing a vast deal of trouble and loss to the government, discouraging reckless speculation, and enabling the industrious settler with moderate means to acquire for himself a clear and unencumbered title to his land.

Meanwhile a controversy sprang up which came near terminating in serious collision with a neighbouring state. By the ordinance of 1787 it was provided that any one of the grand divisions within the limits of the Northwest Territory should be entitled to admission into the Union whenever its population amounted to sixty thousand ; and Michigan having already that number of inhabitants, claimed the right thus granted. The controversy alluded to was in relation to the boundary-line between the latter and Ohio, as established by the ordinance of 1787. Each government claimed a rich and extensive tract as falling within its limits, which was made still more valuable from the proposed terminus of the Wabash and Erie Canal, a work of great promise, being included within it. So much excitement, indeed, prevailed, that both parties sent a military force to the disputed frontier.*

Meanwhile the people of Michigan, having called a Convention and formed a State Constitution, petitioned Congress to be admitted into the Union, claiming as a part of their territory the tract in dispute with Ohio. Congress, however, decided in favour of the latter state, and assigned to Michigan, in place of the fertile strip along her southern border, about twenty-five thousand square miles of barren, mountainous country on the shores of Lake Superior.†

Stevens T. Mason was elected the first governor under the new organization. Mistress of her own legislation, and left to her own energies,

* The ordinance of 1787 declared that not less than three nor more than five states should be formed from the Northwestern Territory. Four of these have been already organized: Ohio was made a state in 1802; Indiana in 1816; Illinois in 1818; Michigan in 1835; and Wisconsin alone remains to be admitted into the Union.

† Act of Congress.

Michigan started forward rapidly in the career of improvement. By a census of her population taken in 1837, it was found to amount to one hundred and seventy-five thousand, consisting principally of emigrants from New-York and New-England. The existing laws were reformed; new ones, where they were required, were enacted; and a plan of public instruction was adopted, for the general diffusion of education among the people. This last act is one of the greatest importance, and posterity will regard as their greatest benefactors those to whose enlightened forethought they will be indebted for so wise and munificent a system.

In connexion with this subject the following particulars will be found interesting. By the ordinance of 1787, seventy-two sections of land were granted by Congress for the endowment of a University, and to these three sections were afterward added, so that this fund now consists of seventy-five sections, amounting to forty-eight thousand acres. In the Report of the Superintendent of Public Instruction submitted to the Legislature in 1838, it is estimated that these lands will sell for one million of dollars. A state University has therefore been organized, with a number of branches, and the parent or central institution established at Ann Arbor, a pleasant village about forty miles west of Detroit.

We have already remarked that, by the ordinance of 1787, lot number 16 in each township was directed to be reserved for the support of common schools. The quantity of land thus coming to the state for this object is one million, one hundred and forty-eight thousand, one hundred and sixty acres, which, according to a recent estimate made by the superintendent of public instruction, will yield about six millions of dollars. Upon this broad basis a thorough system of common school education has been established, which, if faithfully carried out, will secure to the people of Michigan a high character for intelligence: in connexion with virtuous principles, the only guarantee for the permanence of our free institutions.

The system of internal improvements also requires to be noticed, as showing the enterprising spirit of this youthful state. Three lines of railroads have been projected across the peninsular portion of the state, forming what are called the northern, southern, and middle tracks. The northern line is to commence at Palmer, on the St. Clair, and, running through the counties of St. Clair, La Peer, Genesee, Shiawassee, Clinton, and Ionia, and down the Grand River, is designed to terminate at the Grand Rapids, in Kent county. The southern line, starting from Monroe, and running through the counties of Monroe, Lenawee,

Hillsdale, Branch, St. Joseph, Cass, and Berrien, is intended to end at New-Buffalo, upon Lake Michigan. The middle line will commence at Detroit, and, running through the counties of Wayne, Washtenaw, Jackson, Calhoun, Kalamazoo, and Berrien, is intended to terminate at the mouth of the St. Joseph of Lake Michigan.

Besides these different railroads, the route for a canal has been surveyed, to pass through the counties of Macomb, Oakland, Livingston, Ingham, Eaton, Barry, and Allegan, commencing at Mt. Clemens, and terminating at Naples, on the Kalamazoo River, about a mile from Lake Michigan. A ship-canal has also been projected around the Sault de Ste. Marie, to connect the waters of Lake Superior with those below, and thus open a continuous line of navigation throughout the whole extent of these inland seas.

When these various plans of internal improvement shall have been completed, forming four different lines of communication across the peninsula, the products of every part of the state will be brought within reach of a convenient and profitable market ; giving a new impulse to industry, and increased value to the soil.

The local advantages of Michigan are peculiarly great. In addition to the fertility of her soil, she possesses a lake coast which in extent resembles that of the ocean, and which will afford to her advantages similar to those enjoyed by the states bordering on the Atlantic shore ; and of the future magnitude of this internal commerce we may in some measure judge, by considering its vast increase hitherto : twenty years ago there was not a steamer upon the lakes, and very few sail vessels ; whereas there are now about seventy of the former, and several hundred of the latter. May we not anticipate that, at no distant day, the summer tourist will think as little of making an excursion to the head of Lake Superior as he now does of visiting Niagara or Quebec ?

The agricultural industry of the state has, on the whole, kept pace with its improvements in other respects. Paper speculation did indeed, for a while, monopolize everybody's attention ; but sounder views now prevail, and straightforward industry is found to be the surest and best, and for the most part the only road to wealth. Owing to the neglect of cultivation during the speculating mania, the great addition made to the transitory population by the influx of new settlers, and the consequently increased demand for articles from abroad, Michigan became largely indebted to the East. But these evils have been since corrected, and the western farmer is now in a condition to pay for the foreign merchandise he may need with the products of his soil. Instead of being obliged to import wheat for her own consumption, this state has now a large and rapidly-increasing annual surplus for exportation.

We here conclude our brief account of this young but advancing territory. We have seen it in the infancy of its settlement, under the blighting effects of feudal institutions similar to those existing in France at that period, being then little more than a mere ranging-ground for the Jesuit missionary and the fur-trader, a waste roamed over by the wild beast and the savage, and designedly kept in this state as a shelter for the fur-bearing animals. We have seen the French banner supplanted by the red cross of England, without producing any material change in the condition of the country; and, finally, we have seen the stars and stripes of our own republic planted on the soil, and witnessed in the extraordinary improvements which have since taken place the wonder-working energies of our free institutions.

APPENDIX.

NOTE A., page 32.

"*Memoir of the Men and Provisions necessary for the Vessels which the King intends to send into Canada.*

"To perform the voyage which the king our sovereign lord desires to have made to Canada, it must go, at the latest, in the middle of May, and must have the number of persons and ships hereinafter mentioned, to be increased or lessened as M. Le Connetable (the prime minister) shall think proper.

"It will be requisite to have, as well for guarding the ships that will remain there, as for the equipment of several boats which will be wanted to go into the various streams and rivers, 120 mariners:

"Also forty men of war; harquebusiers:

"Also thirty carpenters, as well of ships as of houses, and sawyers who work lengthways:

"Ten master masons, who can be assisted by those of the country who will serve them:

"Three men who can make lime:

"Three makers of tiles:

"Two coalmen, to make charcoal:

"Four master farriers, each having a forge and two servants, with two locksmiths:

"Four smiths, to search and ascertain if there be any mine of iron, and to make forges and work iron there

"To take at least six vine-dressers and six labourers:

"Three barbers, and each a servant:

"Two apothecaries, with each a servant, to examine and see the useful qualities of the herbs:

"A physician and a servant:

"Two goldsmiths who are lapidaries, with their necessary utensils, and each a servant:

"Two master tailors and two master hosiers, and each a servant:

"Two joiners and two servants, with their tools:

"Two master rope-makers and two servants, because there is hemp to make cordage:

"Four cannoniers at least, and the men-of-war will make use of these when need requires:

"Six churchmen, with all things necessary for divine service: in all 276 men; to be victualled for two years at least, that if the ships which shall be sent there next year should not arrive, those now going may not want food.

"These victuals must be well made, and so good as to last all this time; and there must be some of the dry wines of Spain.

"These victuals may cost ten sols a month for each man, which, for the 276 men for twenty-four months, will amount to 33,120 livres.

"They must also be furnished with clothes, beds, coverings, and all other necessaries for two or three years; and they must leave some money behind for their wives and children.

"Therefore they must be paid in advance for fifteen or sixteen months, and this will cost at least, one with the other, 100 sols a month.

"Ten tons of iron, which will cost fifty livres.

"Eight or ten prises of salt, as well for the people of the

country, who very much value it, as for those of the ships. This will cost in Brittany sixty sols for each prise.

"Four milliers yards of common linen, as well for the natives as for the ships.

"Three hundred pieces of crezeaus for natives and ships.

"Also millstones, to make water-mills, wind-mills, and hand-mills.

"They must also carry out as many as possible of all manner and kinds of domestic beasts and birds, as well to do the work as to breed in the country, and all sorts of grains and seeds.

"For their passage there must be at least six ships, of not less than 110 tons, with two barks of forty-five or fifty tons each; these, with the smallest of the six ships, will remain there, and the other five will return as soon as they have landed the victuals and goods. For the return of these five, each must have twenty men over and above the aforesaid number. They may take in going and coming, and in staying there, five or six months, for which time they must be victualled; and be paid two months on going out, and the remainder on their return.

"There must be munitions of war to land for the forts: artillery, arquebuses, a croc, pikes, halberts, lead, balls, powder, and other things.

"In the ships must be three boats, ready to put out when there, to go out on the streams and rivers.

"All sorts of nail-work, pitch, and tar for the ships.

"The six ships, being from 700 to 800 tons, will cost a crown per ton a month for moleage, or about 900 crowns a month, and for the six months 4900 crowns.

"There must be also provided pay and victuals for 100 men, to bring back the shipping this year, who may be detained six months, which would amount to 1000 livres a month, and therefore, for the six months, 6000 livres.

"Made . . . September, 1538."

I derive this curious paper from the collection of state letters made by Ribier in 1666, and addressed by him to Colbert, the celebrated minister of Louis XIV. This counsellor of state describes Canada as then "a vast country, uncultivated like a desert, and in most places uninhabited, except by demons and wild beasts."

NOTE B., page 35.

Massacres of the Jesuits by the Iroquois.

FATHER HENNEPIN, who was for some time a missionary among the Iroquois, states that the savages believed him to be a conjurer, and a burnished silver chalice which he had in his possession was the subject of much fear. "The Indians," says Père Jerome Lallemand, "fear us as the greatest sorcerers on earth." The first religious mission of the Jesuits to the savages of North America was about the year 1611. Their zeal, and their patient endurance of every sort of privation, evinced the strength and fervour of their faith, which was not unfrequently crowned with the tortures of martyrdom. Père Brebœuf, who had suffered the hardships of the wilderness for twenty years, was at last burned alive, together with his coadjutor, Père Lallemand, upon the shores of Lake Huron. A number of other Jesuits were also put to death by the Iroquois. Among these were Daniel, Garnier, Buteaux, La Riborerde, Liegeouis, Goupil, and Constantin. An account of their privations is given in the work of Père Lallemand, entitled "*Relation de ce qui s'est dans le pays des Hurons,*" 1640

"For bed," says he, "we have nothing but a miserable piece of bark of a tree; for nourishment, a handful or two of corn, either roasted or soaked in water, which seldom satisfies our hunger; and, after all, not venturing to perform even the ceremonies of our religion without being considered as sorcerers." In regard to the results of their exertions, Père Lallemand remarks, "With respect to adult persons in good health, there is little apparent success; on the contrary, there have been nothing but storms and whirlwinds from that quarter."

NOTE C., page 85.

THE following grant, being the first in Detroit, was made by Antoine de Lamothe Cadillac, lord of Bouaget Montdesert, and commandant for the king at Detroit Pont Chartrain.

"His majesty, by his despatches of the 14th, 17th, and 19th June, 1705 and 1706, having given us power to cede the lands of Detroit in the manner which we shall judge good and convenient; We, by virtue of the said power from his majesty, have given, granted, and ceded to Francois Fafard Delorme, interpreter for the king in this place, his heirs and assigns, an extent of land of two arpents in front by twenty in depth, joining on one side of our manor, and on the other Francois Bosseron, and on the south the Grand River; which two arpents in front shall be drawn and alienated in the depth by the course north-northwest; and in case any part short of two arpents shall be found in the alienation, the same quantity shall be furnished to him in another place, not yet ceded, without any expense; which said two arpents in front by twenty in depth the said Francois Fafard, his heirs and assigns, shall hold and enjoy forever, with the privilege of fishing, hunting, and trapping—hares, rabbits, partridges, and pheasants excepted. Said Francois Fafard, his heirs and assigns, shall be bound to pay us, our heirs and assigns, in our castle and principal manor, each year on the 20th of March, for the said habitation, the sum of five livres quit rent and rent, and over and above, for other rights whereof we have divested ourselves, the sum of ten livres in peltries good and merchantable; and when a current money shall be established in this country, the said Francois Fafard shall pay the said rent in said money forever. He shall likewise be obliged to begin to clear and improve the said cession within three months from the date of these presents, in default whereof we shall cede his habitation to whom it may appertain. He, his heirs and assigns, shall be, moreover, obliged to comply with the following charges, claims, and conditions, to wit: to come and carry, plant or help to plant, a long Maypole before the door of our principal manor on the first day of May in every year; and if he fail, he shall pay us three livres in money or good peltries; he shall likewise be obliged to come and grind his grain in the mills which we have or shall have hereafter, on paying for the right of grinding, whatever kind the grain may be, eight pounds weight to the bushel; and in case he shall sell his habitation in the whole or in part, he shall be obliged to inform us of it, and we reserve to ourselves the preference, at the price and sum which may be offered him; and, on the same condition, lawful and permitted, he shall not sell, cede, or transfer it by mortgage but with our consent, he being subject to the public charges and servitudes, as also to the fees for right of alienation.

Said Francois Fafard shall not be permitted during ten years to work, or cause any person to work, directly or indirectly, at the profession and trade of a blacksmith, locksmith, armorer, or brewer, without a permit under our hand; reserving, besides, the timber which may be wanted for the fortifications, and for the construction of boats or other vessels. Said Francois Fafard may send down to Montreal, or other places of the lower colony, all the articles he pleases, in as large a quantity as he chooses; and bring from thence merchandise and other effects, in as large a quantity as he chooses, on the condition that he shall sell his said effects and merchandises by himself only, or by other inhabitants of this place, but not by *engagées* or clerks, or foreigners or strangers, not established residents in this place with their family, on pain of confiscation and loss of said effects and merchandises; and in case the said Francois Fafard shall sell, cede, or transfer his habitation in the whole to a foreigner, or another not established in this place, the possessor or purchaser of said habitation in any manner, whatever he may be or become, shall be liable to the same quit rent and rent as the said Francois Fafard; and if the said Francois Fafard sells, cedes, or transfers part of his habitation to a foreigner, the purchaser, in whatever manner he be or become such, shall be obliged to pay us, our heirs and assigns forever, in proportion of the said rent and quit rent; and besides, over and above, for the rights whereof we have divested ourselves, the sum of ten livres for each year, on the 20th day of March. Said Francois Fafard shall not be permitted to sell or trade away brandy to the Indians, on pain of confiscation and loss of his habitation, and of the brandy found thereon, or effects received for the same; and if the said purchaser of the whole or of part is an inhabitant, and pays the sum of ten livres for the rights whereof we have divested ourselves, he shall pay us only the quit rent and rents of his acquisition, and not the sum of ten livres over and above; and if the habitation of the said Francois Fafard passes into other hands, in whatever manner it may be, and he be or become proprietor of another piece of ground, house, or habitation, the said Francois Fafard shall pay us, our heirs and assigns forever, the sum of ten livres for the rights whereof we have divested ourselves, besides the quit rent and rent of the habitation, piece of ground, or house; and in case the said Francois Fafard remains without possession of any land, house, or habitation, he shall be divested of all the privileges to him granted by this present cession. In consideration, generally, of all the claims, charges, and conditions aforesaid towards us, our heirs and assigns, the said Francois Fafard, his heirs and assigns, shall hold and enjoy the said cession; shall sell and trade as well with the French as with the Indians, conforming himself to the regulations and to the orders of his majesty.

Done at Fort Pontchartrain, 10th of March, 1707.

LAMOTHE CADILLAC.

These grants were generally required to be confirmed by the King of France; but, from certain circumstances existing at that period, only three legal grants were made under the French government. To some of these tracts cessions in the rear were subsequently added. Grants were afterward made to French citizens by Bellestre and other of the French commandants; but it appears that these were unauthorized, and were never confirmed by the King of France.

Note D, page 86.

The subjoined petition from sundry inhabitants of Detroit, to stay a trespass on a mill, exhibits the mode of legal proceeding in Michigan under the French domination.

"To Messrs. De Celoron, knight of the royal and military order of St. Louis, commandant for the king at Fort Detroit, and Landrieve, doing the duty of commissary and deputy intendant of New-France in the said place,

"The inhabitants of Detroit humbly represent to you, gentlemen, that the mill situated on the farm of Claude Campeau is of an indispensable necessity and convenience to the public. They have heard that the named Cabacier, an inhabitant of Detroit, was seeking the means to have it demolished, under the pretext that the corner of his meadow was inundated by the said mill. It is easily seen that it is in a spirit of *incompatibility* and contradiction towards his neighbours; for in summer his meadow is dry, and in winter the water has its natural course, the said mill not going on account of the ice. This mill was constructed by the consent of M. De Boisherbert, formerly commandant in this fort, as a thing useful to the public, and a long time before the cession of the land of the said Cabacier. If this mill had given any prejudice to the meadow which is alongside of his land, the first proprietors would not have failed to make representations on that subject. The said mill has always existed till now without any interruption, it being, besides, erected on the land of its proprietor.

"This being considered, may it please you, gentlemen, taking into view the public advantage and convenience, to order that the said mill shall continue as before; it being, besides, the only one handy to this fort, and which goes the greatest part of the year: to forbid the said Cabacier and all others to attempt any depredation on the said mill, or to trouble the owner, on pain of damages, costs, and interest, and you shall do justice.

"Having seen the above, and no title having appeared to us, we order that the parties do apply to the governor and the intendant; and the mill shall remain in its present situation until the decision of the governor and the intendant is had.

"Done at Detroit, 30th June, 1753.

"LANDRIEVE, CELORON.

"After having seen the foregoing petition, we order that the named Campeaux be in peaceable possession of the said mill, having given due regard to the opinion of Messrs. Celoron and Landrieve.

"Done at Montreal, 22d August, 1753.

"DU QUESNE."

NOTE E, page 176.

A TREATY of peace between the United States of America and the tribes of Indians called the Wyandots, Delawares, Shawnees, Ottawas, Chippewas, Pottawatamies, Miamis, Eell River, Weeas, Kickapoos, Kankashaws, and Kaskaskies.

To put an end to a destructive war, to settle all controversies, and to restore harmony and a friendly intercourse between the said United States and Indian tribes: Anthony Wayne, major-general commanding the army of the United States, and sole commissioner for the good purposes above-mentioned, and the said tribes of Indians by their sachems, chiefs, and warriors, met together at Greenville, the headquarters of the said army, have agreed on the following articles, which, when ratified by the president, with the advice and consent of the Senate of the United States, shall be binding on them and the said Indian tribes.

Article 1. Henceforth all hostilities shall cease; peace is hereby established, and shall be perpetual; and a friendly intercourse shall take place between the said United States and Indian tribes.

Article 2. All prisoners shall on both sides be returned. The Indians, prisoners to the United States, shall be immediately set at liberty. The people of the United States still remaining prisoners among the Indians shall be delivered up, in ninety days from the date hereof, to the general or commanding officer at Greenville, Fort Wayne, or Fort Defiance; and ten chiefs of the said tribes shall remain at Greenville as hostages until the delivery of the prisoners shall be effected.

Article 3. The general boundary-line between the lands of the United States and the lands of the said Indian tribes shall begin at the mouth of Wyahoga River, and run thence up the same to the portage between that and the Tuscarora branch of the Muskingum; thence down that branch to the Great Miami River, running into the Ohio at or near which Kerk stood, Loromie's store, and where commences the portage between the Miami of the Ohio and St. Mary's River, which is a branch of the Miami which runs into Lake Erie; thence a westerly course to Fort Recovery, which stands on a branch of the Wabash; thence southwesterly in a direct line to the Ohio, so as to intersect that river opposite the mouth of Kentuky or Cattawa River. And, in consideration of the peace now established, of the goods formerly received from the United States, of those now to be delivered, and of the yearly delivery of goods now stipulated to be made hereafter, and to indemnify the United States for the injuries and expenses they have sustained during the war, the said Indian tribes do hereby cede and relinquish forever all their claims to the lands lying eastwardly and southwardly of the general boundary-line now described; and those lands, or any part of them, shall never hereafter be made a cause or pretence, on the part of the said tribes, or any of them, of war or injury to the United States, or any of the people thereof.

And for the same considerations, and as an evidence of the returning friendship of the said Indian tribes, of their confidence in the United States, and desire to provide for their accommodation, and for that convenient intercourse which will be beneficial to both parties, the said Indian tribes do also cede to the United States the following pieces of land, to wit: (1.) One piece of land six miles square, at or near Loromie's store before mentioned: (2.) One piece two miles square, at the head of the navigable water or landing on the St. Mary's River, near Girty's town: (3.) One piece six miles square, at the head of the navigable water of the Au Glaize River: (4.) One piece six miles square, at the confluence of the Au Glaize and Miami River, where Fort Defiance now stands: (5.) One piece six miles square, at or near the confluence of the Rivers St. Mary's and St. Joseph's, where Fort Wayne now stands, or near it: (6.) One piece two miles square, on the Wabash River, at the end of the portage from the Miami of the Lake, and about eight miles westward from Fort Wayne: (7.) One piece six miles square, at the Ouatanon, or old Weea towns on the Wabash River: (8.) One piece twelve miles square, at the British Fort on the Miami of the Lake, at the foot of the Rapids: (9.) One piece six miles square, at the mouth of the said river, where it empties into the lake: (10.) One piece six miles square, upon Sandusky Lake, where a fort formerly stood: (11.) One piece two miles square, at the lower Rapids of Sandusky River: (12.) The Post of Detroit, and all the land to the north, the west, and the south of it, of which the Indian title has been extinguished by gifts or grants to the French or English governments; and so much more land to be annexed to the District of Detroit as shall be comprehended between the River Rosine on the south, Lake St. Clair on the north, and a line, the general course whereof shall be six miles distant from the west end of Lake Erie and Detroit River: (13.) The post of Michilimackinac, and all the land on the island on which that post stands, and the main land adjacent, of which the Indian title has been extinguished by gifts or grants to the French or English governments; and a piece of land on the main to tne north of the island, to measure six miles on Lake Huron, or the strait between Lake Huron and Michigan, and to extend three miles back from the water of the lake or strait; and also the island de Bois Blanc, being an extra and voluntary gift of the Chippewa nation: (14.) One piece of land of six miles square, at the mouth of Chikajo River, emptying into the southwest end of Lake Michigan, where a fort formerly stood: (15.) One piece twelve miles square, at or near the mouth of the Illinois River, emptying into the Mississippi: (16.) One piece six miles square, at the old Piorias Fort and village, near the south end of the Illinois Lake, on said Illinois River; and whenever the United States shall think proper to survey and mark the boundaries of the land hereby ceded to them, they shall give timely notice thereof to the said tribes of Indians, that they may appoint some of their wise chiefs to attend, and see that the lines are run according to the terms of the treaty.

And the said Indian tribes will allow to the people of the United States a free passage by land and by water, as one and the other shall be found convenient, through their country, along the chain of posts herein before mentioned; that is to say, from the commencement of the portage aforesaid at or near Loromie's store, thence along the said portage to the St. Mary's, and down the same to Fort Wayne, and then down the Miami to Lake Erie. Again, from the commencement of the portage at or near Loromie's store along the portage; from thence to the River Au Glaize, and down the same to its junction with the Miami at Fort Defiance. Again, from the commencement of the portage to the Sandusky River, and down the same to Sandusky Bay and Lake Erie; and from Sandusky to the post which shall be taken at or near the foot of the Rapids of the Miami of the Lake, and from thence to Detroit. Again, from the mouth of Chikajo to the commencement of the portage between that river and the Illinois, and down the Illinois River to the Mississippi; also from Fort Wayne along the portage aforesaid which leads to the Wabash, and then down the Wabash to the Ohio. And the said Indian tribes will also allow to the people of the United States the free use of the harbours and mouths of rivers along the lakes adjoining the Indian lands, for sheltering vessels and boats, and liberty to land their cargoes when necessary for their safety.

Article 4. In consideration of the peace now established, and of the cessions and relinquishments of land made in the preceding article by the said tribes of Indians, and to manifest the liberality of the United States as the great means of rendering this peace strong and perpetual, the

United States relinquish their claims to all other Indian lands northward of the River Ohio, eastward of the Mississippi, and westward and southward of the great lakes, and the waters uniting them, according to the boundary-line agreed on by the United States and the King of Great Britain in the treaty of peace made between them in the year one thousand seven hundred and eighty-three.

But from this relinquishment by the United States the following tracts of land are explicitly excepted :

1st. The tract of one hundred and fifty thousand acres near the Rapids of the River Ohio, which has been assigned to General Clarke for the use of himself and his warriors.

2d. The Post of St. Vincennes, on the River Wabash, and the lands adjacent, of which the Indian title has been extinguished.

3d. The lands at all other places in possession of the French people, and other white settlers among them, of which the Indian title has been extinguished, as mentioned in the third article ; and,

4th. The Post of Fort Massae, towards the mouth of the Ohio. To which several parcels of land so excepted, the said tribes relinquish all the title and claim which they or any of them may have.

And for the same considerations, and with the same views as above mentioned, the United States now deliver to the said Indian tribes a quantity of goods to the value of twenty thousand dollars, the receipt whereof they do hereby acknowledge ; and henceforward every year forever, the United States will deliver, at some convenient place northward of the River Ohio, like useful goods, suited to the circumstances of the Indians, to the value of nine thousand five hundred dollars, reckoning that value as the first cost of the goods in the city or place of the United States where they shall be procured. The tribes to which those goods are to be annually delivered, and the proportions in which they are to be delivered, are the following: 1st. To the Wyandots the amount of one thousand dollars 2d. To the Delawares the amount of one thousand dollars. 3d. To the Shawnees the amount of one thousand dollars. 4th. To the Miamis the amount of one thousand dollars. 5th. To the Ottawas the amount of one thousand dollars. 6th. To the Chippewas the amount of one thousand dollars. 7th. To the Pottawatamies the amount of one thousand dollars. 8th. To the Kickapoo, Lorra, Eell River, Kankashaws, and Kaskaskias tribes, the amount of five hundred dollars each.

Provided, That if either of the said tribes shall hereafter, at an annual delivery of their share of the goods aforesaid, desire that a part of their annuity should be furnished in domestic animals, implements of husbandry, and other utensils convenient for them, and in compensation to useful artificers, who may reside with or near them, and be employed for their benefit, the same shall, at the subsequent annual deliveries, be furnished accordingly.

Article 5. To prevent any misunderstanding about the Indian lands relinquished by the United States in the fourth article, it is now explicitly declared that the meaning of that relinquishment is this: The Indian tribes who have a right to those lands are quietly to enjoy them, hunting, planting, and dwelling thereon so long as they please, without any molestation from the United States; but when those tribes, or any of them, shall be disposed to sell their lands, or any part of them, they are to be sold only to the United States; and, until such sales, the United States will protect all the said Indian tribes in the quiet enjoyment of their lands against all citizens of the United States, and against all other white persons who intrude upon the same; and the said Indian tribes again acknowledge themselves to be under the protection of the United States, and no other power whatever.

Article 6. If any citizen of the United States, or any other white person or persons, shall presume to settle upon the lands now relinquished by the United States, such citizen or other person shall be out of the protection of the United States; and the Indian tribe on whose lands the settlement shall be made, may drive off the settler, or punish him in such a manner as they shall think fit; and because such settlements, made without the consent of the United States, will be injurious to them as well as to the Indians, the United States shall be at liberty to break them up, and remove and punish the settlers as they shall think proper, and so effect that protection of the Indian lands herein before stipulated.

Article 7. The said tribes of Indians, parties to this treaty, shall be at liberty to hunt within the territory and lands which they have now ceded to the United States without hinderance or molestation, so long as they demean themselves peaceably, and offer no injury to the people of the United States.

Article 8. Trade shall be opened with the said Indian tribes; and they do hereby respectively engage to afford protection to such persons, with their property, as shall be duly licensed to reside among them, for the purpose of trade, and to their agents and servants; but no person shall be permitted to reside at any of their towns or hunting-camps as a trader, who is not furnished with a license for that purpose under the hand and seal of the superinendent of the department northwest of the Ohio, or such other persons as the President of the United States shall authorize to examine such licenses, to the end that the said Indians may not be imposed on in their trade; and if any licensed trader shall abuse his privilege by unfair dealing, upon complaint and proof thereof his license shall be taken from him, and he shall be farther punished according to the laws of the United States. And if any person shall intrude himself as a trader without such license, the said Indians shall take and bring him before the superintendent or his deputy, to be dealt with according to law; and, to prevent impositions by forged licenses, the said Indians shall, at least once a year, give information to the superintendent or his deputies of the names of the traders residing among them.

Article 9. Lest the firm peace and friendship now established should be interrupted by the misconduct of individuals, the United States and the said Indian tribes agree that, for injuries done by individuals on either side, no private revenge or retaliation shall take place; but, instead thereof, complaint shall be made by the party injured to the other: by the said Indian tribes or any of them to the President of the United States, or the superintendent by him appointed; and by the superintendent, or other person appointed by the president, to the principal chiefs of the Indian tribes, or of the tribe to which the offender belongs; and such prudent measures shall then be pursued as shall be necessary to preserve the said peace and friendship unbroken, until the Legislature (or Great Council) of the United States shall make other equitable provision in the case to the satisfaction of both parties. Should any Indian tribes meditate a war against the United States or either of them, and the same shall come to the knowledge of the before-mentioned tribes or either of them, they do hereby engage to give notice thereof to the general or officer commanding the troops of the United States at the nearest post. And should any tribe, with hostile intentions against the United States or either of them, attempt to pass through their country, they will endeavour to prevent the same, and, in like manner, give information of such attempt to the general or officer commanding as soon as possible, that all causes of mistrust and suspicion may be avoided between them and the United States.

In like manner, the United States shall give notice to the said Indian tribes of any harm that may be meditated against them, or either of them, that shall come to their knowledge, and do all in their power to hinder and prevent the same, that the friendship between them may be uninterrupted.

Article 10. All other treaties heretofore made between the United States and the said Indian tribes, or any of them, since the treaty of 1783 between the United States and Great Britain, that come within the provisions of this treaty, shall henceforth cease and become void.

Done at Greenville, in the territory of the United States, northwest of the River Ohio, on the third day of August, one thousand seven hundred and ninety-five.

ANTHONY WAYNE (L.S.).

NOTE F, page 200.

By WILLIAM HULL, Brigadier-general and Commander-in-chief of the Northwestern Army of the United States.

A PROCLAMATION.

Inhabitants of Canada:

After thirty years of peace and prosperity, the United States have been driven to arms. The injuries and aggressions, the insults and indignities of Great Britain, have left them no alternative but manly resistance or unconditional submission. The army under my command has invaded your country, and the standard of the Union now waves over the territory of Canada. To the peaceable, unoffending inhabitants it brings neither danger nor difficulty. I come to find enemies, not to make them; I come to protect, not to injure you. Separated by an immense ocean and an extensive wilderness from Great Britain, you have no participation in her councils, no interest in her conduct; you have felt her tyranny, you have seen her injustice; but I do not ask you to revenge the one or to redress the other. The United States are sufficiently powerful to afford every security consistent with their rights and your expectations. I tender you the invaluable blessing of civil, political, and religious liberty, and their necessary result, individual and general prosperity. That liberty which gave decision to our councils and energy to our conduct in a struggle for independence, and which conducted us safe and triumphantly through the stormy period of the Revolution. That liberty which has raised us to an elevated rank among the nations of the world, and which afforded us a greater measure of peace, and security of wealth, and improvement, than ever fell to the lot of any country. In the name of my country, and by the authority of government, I promise you protection to your persons, property, and rights. Remain at your homes; pursue your peaceful and customary avocations; raise not your hand against your brethren. Many of your fathers fought for the freedom and independence we now enjoy. Being children, therefore, of the same family with us, and heirs to the same heritage, the arrival of an army of friends must be hailed by you with a cordial welcome. You will be emancipated from tyranny and oppression, and restored to the dignified station of freemen. Had I any doubt of eventual success, I might ask your assistance; but I do not; I come prepared for every contingency. I have a force which will look down all opposition, and that force is the vanguard of a much greater. If, contrary to your own interest and the just expectation of my country, you should take part in the approaching contest, you will be considered and treated as enemies, and the horrors and calamities of war will stalk before you. If the barbarous and savage policy of Great Britain be pursued, and the savages be let loose to murder our citizens and butcher our women and children, this war will be a war of extermination. The first stroke of the tomahawk, the first attempt with the scalping-knife, will be the sequel of one indiscriminate scene of desolation. No white man found fighting by the side of an Indian will be taken prisoner; instant destruction will be his lot. If the dictates of reason, duty, justice, and humanity cannot prevent the employment of a force which respects no rights and knows no wrong, it will be prevented by a severe and relentless system of retaliation. I doubt not your courage and firmness; I will not doubt your attachment to liberty. The United States offer you peace, liberty, and security; your choice lies between these and war, slavery and destruction. Choose, then, but choose wisely; and may He who knows the justice of our cause, and who holds in his hands the fate of nations, guide you to a result the most compatible with your rights and interests, your peace and happiness.

By the general, A. P. Hull,
Capt. of the 13th U. S. Reg't. of Infantry and Aiddecamp.
Headquarters, Sandwich, July 12th, 1812.

THE END.

www.ingramcontent.com/pod-product-compliance
Lightning Source LLC
LaVergne TN
LVHW010241110826
845151LV00004B/1360

* 9 7 8 1 4 2 5 5 2 3 6 9 5 *